The Juiceman®'s Power of Juicing

The Juiceman®'s Power of Juicing

Jay Kordich

wm

WILLIAM MORROW
An Imprint of HarperCollinsPublishers

A hardcover edition of this book was published in 1992 by William Morrow, an imprint of HarperCollins Publishers.

THE JUICEMAN®'S POWER OF JUICING. Copyright © 1992 by Jay Kordich. All rights reserved. Printed in the United States of America. No part of this book may be used or reproduced in any manner whatsoever without written permission except in the case of brief quotations embodied in critical articles and reviews. For information address HarperCollins Publishers, 10 East 53rd Street, New York, NY 10022.

HarperCollins books may be purchased for educational, business, or sales promotional use. For information please write: Special Markets Department, HarperCollins Publishers, 10 East 53rd Street, New York, NY 10022.

First paperback edition published 2007.

Designed by Richard Oriolo

The Library of Congress has catalogued the hardcover edition as follows:

Kordich, Jay.
The juiceman®'s power of juicing /
by Jay Kordich.
p. cm.
Includes bibliographical references.
ISBN 0-688-11443-1
1. Vegetable juices. 2. Fruit juices.
3. Natural foods. I. Title.
RM236.K67 1992
613.2'6—dc20 91-42984
CIP

ISBN: 978-0-06-115370-9 (pbk.)
ISBN-10: 0-06-115370-2

12 13 14 15 RRD 20 19 18 17 16 15 14 13 12

To my beloved parents,
Jack and Vica Kordich

Acknowledgments

There are so many wonderful people in my life who have helped me and provided encouragement and support. But I want to single out just a few here, to thank them from the bottom of my heart.

This book would not have happened without my wife, Linda. She provided the inspiration, perspiration, and prodding to make a twenty-year dream come true. There are no words to express my love and gratitude to her and my children.

A thousand thanks go to Shirley Lemire, who did an excellent job editing our seminar lecture material and videotapes.

To Steve Cesari and Bob Lamson and the wonderful people at JM Marketing: thank you, thank you, thank you!

Huge thanks to Eric Yaverbaum and all the great people at Jericho Promotions—both for the excellent job they do championing "The Juiceman" and for introducing me to Bill Adler, my book agent, a "real pro!" The best of the best!

To Nick Goyak, my attorney, and Bill Miller, my CPA, deep gratitude for guiding me through troubled waters.

I owe a great deal to Steve Edelman and Sharon Anderson of the television show Good Company in Minneapolis–St. Paul, and to their former producer, Katie Davis, who believed in the cause and helped me reach millions of people.

A very special thanks to Brenda Wolsey, B.S., nutritionist with JM Marketing for her careful research and valuable comments.

Thanks to Will Schwalbe, my editor at William Morrow and Company. How lucky can you get?

And enormous thanks to Mary Goodbody, a brilliant wordsmith. She has a beautiful way with words and helped me say everything just the way I wanted to say it. Thanks for all your work, your grace under pressure, and your good cheer!

A very important thank you goes to Dan Reilly for insisting that I talk to Rick Cesari before signing any agreement to promote "The Juiceman®" Juicer.

Which leads to my unbounded gratitude to and admiration for Rick Cesari, a very special person in my life. His talent created the synergy that got me where I am today.

And what can I tell you about Jack Lee? Friend, adviser extraordinaire, master diplomat, and confidant. Here is a man whom everyone loves . . . but no one more than I. There is no way to express how grateful I am.

And I owe my most sincere thanks to all of the people around the world who have written to me, called me, stopped me on the street, attended my lectures, and communicated to me their love of juicing and how it has changed their lives. The strength and joy that these words and letters have given me are immense. Thank you all . . . and keep juicing!

Contents

Introduction:
Welcome to Juicing

My sincerest wish is that this book changes your life. The change may be gradual or rapid, it may be barely noticeable or startlingly monumental. But once you begin including fresh juices in your daily diet I promise you will feel better and look better, and most likely you will be healthier too. Vegetable and fruit juices are packed with concentrated nutrients, and simply by drinking a few glasses of delicious juice every day, you supply your body with many of the essential elements that contribute to its strength and general well-being.

What could be better? These juices are pure and natural. You make them yourself in your own kitchen, so you know precisely what is in them. They take minutes to prepare and minutes to drink, rendering them the ultimate fast food. Within weeks, your skin will be glowing and your hair shining with renewed vitality. Even better, you will probably feel more energetic than before, ready to face everyday challenges with enthusiasm and vigor.

I have been juicing for nearly fifty years. I also eat a diet that consists mostly of raw foods. I am in terrific health and have the same energy I had in my thirties and forties. And I am sixty-nine years old. I truly believe that juices have contributed more than anything else to my good health and optimistic outlook. Please keep in mind that I am not advocating a drastic change in your diet, but I am urging you to drink juice regularly as a healthful supplement to your daily meals, and while doing so to consider the fat and sodium count in the rest of the food you consume. The beauty of drinking juices every day is that they make this ridiculously simple.

The Juiceman's Power of Juicing can help you achieve the healthful eating habits I recommend while discovering the fun and creativity of juicing. These pages are filled with information both for the reader who is merely curious about juicing as well as for the reader who is already committed to a healthful diet and interested in an even healthier one. In other words, regardless of how serious you are about juicing, this book has something for you.

Let's start with the recipes. My wife, Linda, and I have assembled more than a hundred recipes for fresh, frothy vegetable and fruit juices. Thumb through the pages containing the recipes—aren't you tempted to try a refreshing glass of Jay's World Famous Lemonade, Tropical Sunset, Tangerine

Sky, or another delicious, exotic juice drink? Have you tasted carrot juice in a health food store? Sweet, isn't it? Try making it yourself and discover how even more delicious it is when freshly made and mixed with apple juice. By the way, Carrot-Apple Juice is my personal all-time favorite!

And there is lots, lots more. Turn to Chapter 5, "Fruits and Vegetables—and Why They Are So Good for You." Here I discuss many of my favorites and why they are perfect for juicing. Each entry includes the unique health benefits of each fruit and vegetable as well as practical buying and storing information. The next chapter is on vitamins and minerals, and it provides a handy cross-reference for the nutrients found in the fruits and vegetables discussed in Chapter 5 while supplying you with a good understanding of these often baffling body builders.

Then Chapter 7 outlines more than forty common ailments and more serious ailments that may be helped or possibly avoided by drinking fresh juices. Don't misunderstand. Juices are *not* medicine. They are pure and nutritious foods that feed the body with the vitamins and minerals it needs to stay healthy. This chapter also includes juices that are beneficial as beauty aids, for example, for shiny hair and wrinkle-free skin.

I hope you begin juicing right away. But before you do, I suggest you take stock of what equipment you need to turn your kitchen into what I call a "natural kitchen." Don't worry; other than the juicer, there is not much—you probably already own a number of the items I suggest in Chapter 3, "Setting Up a Natural Kitchen." To be sure, read these pages. The chapter is full of helpful hints for converting your kitchen into the focal point for your healthful, nutritious eating.

Many of you may want to explore the power of juicing in more depth than is described in the opening chapters of the book. For you, I have written Chapter 8, "Juice as a Way of Life." This chapter outlines my personal dietary habits, and believe me, I have pulled no punches when it comes to exhorting my prejudices and preferences. I itemize the foods I would like to see everyone eliminate—or at least cut back—from his or her diet. All this information is qualified by logical and sound nutritional reasoning. Best of all, making your diet more healthful is easy and pleasurable the minute you decide to include fresh juices on a daily basis.

There is another bonus to juicing: It's a great way to lose weight naturally without feeling deprived. Vegetable and fruit juices are low in calories and are practically fat-free. They taste superb and fill you up so that you are not tempted to down a handful of cookies or a candy bar. Read through Chapter 9, "Juicing for Weight Loss," and then enjoy drinking my delicious juices while feeling the pounds melt away.

I think juicing is a magnificent way to feed the body with valuable vitamins and minerals. You may still have questions about integrating fresh vegetable and fruit juices into your life that weren't answered to your satisfaction, so I end this book by answering the most common questions asked me as I travel around the country teaching people about the power of juicing. I trust after reading this chapter and the ones preceding it you will agree with Linda and me: Juicing is a delicious and easy path toward leading a healthful life. Welcome to the delicious world of juicing.

1

How I Became the Juiceman

When I was a young man in the early 1940s, I ate a lot of meat and played a lot of football. The culmination of my career at the University of Southern California (USC) was the opportunity to play in the Rose Bowl. What a thrill that was! At the time I was barely twenty years old and, with the naïveté and idealism of youth, I honestly thought I saw my life stretching before me as football coach and athletic instructor. How rewarding it would be to help young men learn the value of playing hard, of sportsmanship, and of being champions. Then, out of the blue, I became gravely ill and the doctors told me I might not live.

I am sure you can imagine how a young, apparently healthy man felt with such a dire prognosis. I was devastated, depressed, angry, terrified—but I refused to give up hope. How could this happen? Why was my body—which, as a vigorous athlete I practically worshipped—betraying me? I began reading everything I could get my hands on about illness and cures in both the conventional and alternative medical press. When I came across some literature about a German doctor named Max Gerson, I felt I was onto something. Dr. Gerson had recently emigrated to the United States and was treating patients in New York City with freshly made carrot juice and other natural foods, an idea that appealed to me. The doctors I had been consulting could not assure me a complete recovery, and so I packed my bags and headed east.

Once in Manhattan, I began a regimen of drinking thirteen glasses of carrot-apple juice every day, beginning at 6:00 A.M. and repeating the dosage every hour until early evening. Two and a half years later I was a well man. But more than being physically healthy, I was forever changed. As I regained my health, I made a personal commitment to dedicate my life to spreading the word about the power of juicing.

That was nearly fifty years ago and I have not veered from my chosen path. Now, after decades of barely getting by financially, I have developed and marketed a commercial juicer that bears my name, I have appeared on countless television and radio shows, I have conducted numerous national seminars, I have produced training videos and audiotapes—and I have written this book.

But how did I get from Dr. Gerson's Park Avenue clinic in the late 1940s to writing a book about juicing in the 1990s? It wasn't profit that motivated me, but teaching others about juicing. As I saw it, the logical way to do this was to demonstrate juicers to the public. Shortly after leaving the clinic in New York and returning to my native Los Angeles, I joined a company called the Norwalk Food Factory. It produced a juicer endorsed by Dr. Norman Walker, a man who was to become one of my most cherished mentors and who espoused many of the nutritional beliefs I have adopted over the years. I did not sell the juicer door-to-door, but instead followed telephone leads and inquiries, demonstrating the machine in home kitchens throughout Southern California. Many of our customers were shut-ins who desired more healthful diets and were intrigued by the idea of the juicer. With Dr. Walker's informational pamphlet and my own convictions, I sold a good number of machines. Regardless of whether I made a sale or not, I was repeatedly gratified and excited by the response to that first sip of carrot juice or fresh pineapple juice. To this day, the look on someone's face as he experiences the deliciousness of juice still awes and inspires me. But I yearned to reach even more people, and so after a few years and a lot of long, hard thought, I decided to switch companies and demonstrate a less costly juicer in department stores.

I assembled tables piled high with fresh vegetables and fruits in Woolworth's and J. J. Newbury's in Los Angeles and demonstrated the juicer to anyone who walked by. In those postwar days, health food stores were few and far between, even in sunny California, but so many customers seemed fascinated by the juicer and the juices, I decided to try my luck at home shows and country fairs. Meanwhile, I made contact with a buyer at Abraham & Straus, a New York department store, and soon found myself crisscrossing the country demonstrating in large department stores, small home shows, and all sorts of fairs. I worked in stores such as Marshall Field's in Chicago, Foley's in Houston, Lazarus Brothers in Cincinnati, Joske's in San Antonio, and The Broadway in Los Angeles. Knowledge about juicing was primitive then, but because these were extremely reputable stores and many of the customers had credit cards, I was able to keep going.

Nevertheless, times were tough. I bought a small pickup with a camper shell to make traveling from town to town and city to city easier. To save on motel costs, I frequently slept in the back of the truck, and I recall one time in particular that typifies my existence in those days. I had just spent ten very long, fruitless days at a fair in Davenport, Iowa, without selling one juicer. It was discouraging, but considering the healthful eating during the 1950s, it was not unusual. Those ten days left me practically penniless, and after heading out of town toward Michigan, my next appointment, I pulled over to the side of a country road, turned off the engine, and crawled into the camper shell to sleep. I quickly realized the temperature had plummeted to below freezing. Those were the days before sleeping bags and other camping gear were made for sub-zero weather, so a broke salesman sleeping in his car had no choice but to pile every item of clothing he owned on top of him and burrow into the laundry like some sort of hibernating animal.

There were other lean times too. My home base was in San Pedro, California, where I grew up the son of Yugoslavian immigrants. As a family we struggled through the Great Depression of the 1930s, raising much of our own food in a small plot behind our house. I had been married and divorced very young, but I had two wonderful boys from that first marriage. Obviously, the dream of a career in football died hard when I became ill, but because my parents had instilled in me a strong sense of working hard for my goals, I never gave up the dream of teaching people about the power of juicing. During those early years I sometimes worked two jobs to keep going, hefting cargo on the Los Angeles docks by day and loading dairy trucks by night. In between times I worked out and showered at a small health club and slept in the back of my truck in the parking lot of the dairy. After a few months, with enough money for gasoline and produce, I hit the road again to demonstrate juicers.

This was how I spent the 1950s and 1960s. As I got better known and as public consciousness rose about the value of a healthful diet, my style of living became a little easier. I began appearing on television shows, which in those days were mostly live. It was on a variety show one day in 1961 in Cincinnati, Ohio, that I, who was born John Kordich, became "Jay the Juiceman." A fellow named Paul Dixon had a very popular local morning show that featured regional talent and short spots on a number of topics. The department store where I demonstrated juicers sponsored the show and asked me to appear as its representative. Television and I hit it off and I soon became something of a regular on *The Paul Dixon Show*. I also grew very fond of Paul, a big, happy-go-lucky fellow who liked partying late into the night and consequently was sometimes bleary-eyed in the morning. On that particular morning, I was waiting in the wings with a large, rolling table loaded with colorful fresh vegetables and fruits. Paul was having a little trouble reading the cue cards and so he glanced in my direction, made out the juicer, the produce, and me, and announced with a big grin, "Ladies and gentlemen, here's Jay the Juiceman!" I accepted the epithet and, as you know, have used it ever since.

By that time, I was working with a company based in Aarburg, Switzerland, named Rotel International that took my advice and designed a juicer that did not rely on centrifugal force to eject the pulp but instead ejected the pulp with the help of a powerful motor. This was the prototype for the machine that today bears my name, and while it eventually took nearly twenty years to perfect the design, I proudly took the early models on the road. I was merely a consultant and salesman for the juicer, but as my relationship with Rotel continued, I finally acquired the import rights to the machine in 1978 and gave it The Juiceman® name.

By the 1970s health food stores were cropping up all around the country. Early in that decade I demonstrated the Rotel juicer at the Natural Living Center in Wilton, Connecticut, and found myself making juices and talking about their benefits for a full hour on Bob Norman's television show in New Haven. Later that afternoon word came back to the Natural Living Center that every health food store in the area had sold out of juicers and more were on order.

Up until that day I had enjoyed appearing on variety shows such as Paul Dixon's but it took this incident to illustrate the force of television. What if I combined the power of the medium with the power of juicing? I could reach the thousands of people I had been trying to reach since the early days with the Norwalk Food Factory juicer. As excited as I was about the idea, it was a concept that did not reach fruition until the 1980s—when it happily proved to be true.

I was pleased to be importing the Rotel juicers and calling them The Juiceman®, and I continued to demonstrate them at health food stores such as the famous Mrs. Gooch's Natural Food Market in Los Angeles and elsewhere around the country. In September 1980 I met a young woman in San Diego. As we chatted, I found out that she was a lifelong vegetarian and that she believed in the power of juicing as much as I did. Linda and I were married on January 11, 1981, a short week after our first "offical" date, and she immediately joined me in my travels as I took the juicer to stores and fairs and local television shows, as well as to the fledgling seminars I was beginning to conduct. My new wife gamely slept in the back of the camper when necessary, even braving those less-than-comfortable accommodations when she was pregnant with our first son, John, who was born in 1984. (Our second son, Jayson, was born in 1986.) Linda stood on the sidelines and watched me, then a man in his early sixties, on his feet all day, talking and joking with customers for eight or ten hours at a stretch. She hated how hoarse I got, how hard the life was, and she urged me to change course. Her planning and perseverance, as well as her faith in me and in our product finally won me a spot on *The Rita Davenport Show* in Phoenix, Arizona.

I think that opportunity catapulted me to a new media height. Suddenly, other television talk show hosts and producers recognized the appeal of the juicer and its message and I was in demand. In the mid 1980s, Linda and I moved to Seattle, Washington, where we teamed up with Lester Gray of *Seattle Today.* Not only was Lester a great TV producer, he understood the power of juicing, and among other shows, he helped me get a booking on *Good Company* in Minneapolis, with husband and wife hosts Steve Adleman and Sharon Anderson. The national respect that show enjoys helped me enormously.

My television career took off, just as the seminars I conducted around the country did. In these I demonstrated the juicer—much as I had all those years in department stores and at county fairs—to folks who wanted to improve their diets with fresh juices. In 1987, Linda and I incorporated The Juiceman and we knew then that the time was right to take our message national. Today a team of trained and dedicated people travel around the country conducting seminars at hotels and other public meeting places, usually talking to a crowd of hundreds of enthusiastic Americans who embrace the power of juicing. I still travel nearly half of every month, giving seminars and making television and radio appearances.

My greatest joy has been meeting people whose lives have been improved because of juicing. From the very earliest days, I have come in contact with the most incredible people, many of whom have shaped my life, giving it rich texture and deep meaning, so that, looking back, I cannot imagine for- going even one of these experiences. Let me give you an example that has long stayed with me.

It was back in the 1960s and I was doing a week-long stint at Joske's Department Store in San Antonio. The juicer I sold in those days cost $139.95, a sizable chunk of money for nearly anyone. Every day, I noticed the same weathered- looking man standing well back in the crowd. Finally, on the last day, he approached me and, because he spoke no En- glish, indicated with hand motions that he wanted to buy a juicer. He pulled $39.95 from a worn wallet, having misun- derstood the price and, perhaps, the currency. What could I do? I communicated that he was short money and he could not buy a machine from Joske's. But, asking him to help me cart my equipment to the parking lot and thus put value on the deal, I offered him a demo model from the back of my truck for his money. He gladly accepted it—and my offer of a lift home. When we reached his house, he invited me in and as I entered the modest one-room abode, I immediately was struck by a large piece of furniture covered with a spotless blanket. The man asked me to sit down and then he pulled the blanket from a lovingly maintained piano. That afternoon I was treated to the most memorable concert of my life. My private customer paid me handsomely with some of the most elegant and heartfelt music I have ever heard.

That, my friends, is the power of juicing: the ability to reach people with a message so clear, so simple, and so straightforward that it strikes a basic chord in us all. Natural, pure juices are delicious and wonderfully healthful, but because they speak directly of the earth and sky, they put us in touch with our most elemental needs, freeing our bodies so that our spirits can reach their full potential with energy and happiness.

2

Why Juice?

These pages contain the knowledge I have acquired during a lifetime of drinking juice and eating raw foods. The past forty years have convinced me that my diet is the best one for maintaining a healthy, vigorous body that functions as well today, when I am sixty-nine, as it did when I was in my thirties and forties.

We all are programmed genetically before birth. In understanding this, I realize that my unique physiological makeup contributes in some degree to my overall good health. But because I believe strongly that we are what we eat, I decided years ago that a diet composed of fresh juices, whole grains, legumes, and organic fruits and vegetables is the key to good health. I consider myself living proof!

This book is not intended as a scientific dissertation. Many of its theories are only now finding credence in the medical community, while still others are not yet considered. I can only share my experience, which solidly forms the foundation of my life and shapes my philosophy.

I believe that if you add juice to your life, you will contribute to your overall cardiovascular health, enhance your physical performance, help lower your blood pressure, sleep better at night—and have more energy and better health than you probably ever dreamed possible.

I travel a lot, demonstrating The Juiceman® juicers and conducting seminars on health and nutrition. Over the years I have talked with thousands of people, many several times as the years went by, and I am happy to report that their enthusiasm and radiant good health clearly show me that I am not the only one benefiting from including juice in the diet. It is not uncommon at all for people to approach me after a seminar or to write me letters with a "miracle" story of how despondent and/or ill they felt before adding juice to their diets. These personal experiences feed my soul just as fresh, chemical-free, and preservative-free foods and juices feed my body.

Every day I nurture the trillions of cells in my body with fresh juices and raw foods. We need fiber—no one can live on juice alone—and I get my fiber by eating around the juicer. The juice always comes first when I am planning what I will eat. After you read this book, begin adding juice to your diet. You will find that the juices are delightful discoveries that pave a palatable and delicious path to good health.

The Benefits of Juice

As I said, we are what we eat. The food we put in our systems determines the health of every cell and organ in our bodies. The human body needs "live" foods to build "live cells." By live foods I mean uncooked fruits and vegetables. Other foods, such as nuts, grains, seeds, and legumes are live foods too. All come directly from the soil and are not first processed by another animal, as are meat, poultry, and fish. For this reason, I consider them live—and full of life.

When we eat fresh fruits and vegetables, our bodies extract as liquid what they need from the fiber, which passes on to the lower digestive tract. For all intents and purposes, the extracted liquid is juice, containing the same elements as the juice you make in your kitchen with the juicer. By drinking juice, you are eliminating a digestive process—extracting the liquid from the fiber—and efficiently supplying the body with nutrients. The juicer separates the juice from the fiber so that what you drink is pulp-free and your body receives the maximum amount of nutrients in minutes. The juice from the juicer is different from bottled, canned, or concentrated juices sold in the supermarket. First, it is absolutely fresh—which is important because nutrients lose a lot of value soon after juicing. Second, juice from the juicer is not pasteurized, which means "cooked," and so is bursting with the living cells I feel are so vital to good health. Finally, fresh juice is absolutely pure, free of additives and preservatives.

Nearly everyone likes the idea of drinking fresh unadulterated juice. Yet many people harbor a common misconception about the role of a juicer. Why, they ask, can't they simply pop the fruit or vegetable into a blender or food processor? The answer is simple. The blender and processor purée the food, making a pulp that is nothing more than a liquefied version of the whole food. The juicer extracts the life-giving juice from the fiber.

One cup of carrot juice contains the equivalent nutrition of four cups of raw, chopped carrots. Made fresh and consumed on the spot, juices, which contain about 95 percent of the food value of the fruit or vegetable, instantly release nourishment to the body through the bloodstream. In the process, the body receives the necessary nutrients: vitamins and minerals. For most people there is then no need whatsoever for supplements. Therefore, incorporating juice into your diet is a purely healthful and natural way to furnish the body with all its nutritional needs.

Vegetable and Fruit Juices

It is important to understand the difference between juices made from fruits and those made from vegetables. When most people purchase a juicer they immediately start juicing fruits. After all, they are used to drinking orange juice and apple juice and are eager to sample the "real" thing. Believe me, nothing compares with apple juice from the juicer—it tastes even more intensely of the apple than the actual fruit. But as delicious as fruit juices are, I tend to be a fruitarian when I eat and a vegetarian when I juice. There are a few reasons why I drink more vegetable than fruit juice, and conversely why I eat more fruits than vegetables.

First, vegetables are harder to digest when eaten whole.

They tend to be bulkier and break down more slowly in the body than fruit does. When I drink vegetable juice, my body absorbs the food immediately.

Second, vegetables are the building blocks of life, responsible for strong, healthy muscles, tissue, glands, and organs. By consuming vegetables in juice form, I am assured that I get nearly 100 percent of the available nutrients, particularly the minerals.

Third, whole fruits are more easily digested than vegetables are and are a good source of fiber. And whole fruits are a lot easier to eat than whole vegetables. You won't have trouble eating a couple of apples in one day, but you may not want to eat a dozen or more carrots. Also, fruits such as pears and apples contain a lot of pectin, a digestive aid that helps regulate the body, and pectin is best absorbed by eating the fruits whole.

Finally, fruits are the revitalizers and cleansers of the body. Although I do drink fruit juices for quick energy, a lift first thing in the morning or during the day, I munch mainly on fresh fruits—apples, peaches, berries, or melon. As I will repeat throughout the book, I drink two glasses of fruit juice and at least four glasses of vegetable juice every day. But you can begin to reap the benefits of juicing by adding just one glass of juice a day to your diet. I suspect you will like the juice so much, you will add two or three before long. And you will feel great and look terrific.

The Most Important Juices

All fruits and vegetables have important roles to play in maintaining good health, but a few stand out above the others. Carrot juice and celery juice will quickly become part of your daily regimen when you start juicing, as will apple juice, a wonderfully versatile juice that bridges the gap between fruits and vegetables, as it is the only one that should be mixed with either.

Leafy greens such as spinach, parsley, lettuce, and sprouts (especially wheatgrass, which you can sprout at home, see pages 204 to 205) are vitally important. Melon juices (including cantaloupe, honeydew, and watermelon) and pineapple juice are especially healthful and effortless to prepare. They can be juiced with the rind, seeds, and all to provide the maximum nutrition available from these sweet, juicy fruits. Finally, citrus juice is a terrific source of vitamin C, a very necessary vitamin our bodies do not store and therefore must replenish every day.

Overall Health Benefits
of Juicing

Drinking freshly made juices and eating enough whole foods to provide adequate fiber is a sensible approach to a healthful diet. But incorporating juice into your life does so much more. The abundance of live, uncooked foods flushes your body of toxins, leaving you feeling refreshed, energized, and relaxed all at the same time. The pure foods make your skin glow, your hair shine, your breath fresh, and your entire system so regulated you will never have to give it another thought. Colds and flu become fewer and farther between; many people report that arthritic joints loosen with renewed flexibility; and gums and teeth become less prone to bleeding and cavities.

And there's more. Research has shown that beta carotene plays a significant role in the prevention of many diseases. In action, it works as an antioxidant, neutralizing harmfully charged molecules known as free radicals. In doing this, beta carotene protects the invaluable genetic blueprint inside each cell, which translates to healthy cells with far less possibility of developing malignancies.

Today, the established medical community urges everyone to consume more vegetables with beta carotene as a guard against an array of cancers. Carrots are a great source of beta carotene, as are the cruciferous vegetables: broccoli, cabbage, cauliflower, spinach, Brussels sprouts, kale, greens, watercress, kohlrabi, and rutabagas. The American Cancer Society recommends three or four servings of these vegetables every week. The society states that the crucifers "might reduce the incidence of colon, stomach and esophageal cancers. In animals, these vegetables have inhibited the effects of carcinogens." Who can argue? I believe juicing is the ideal way to consume these valuable vegetables raw and in quantity so that the important nutrients get right to work.

Chlorophyll is another element that has been proven valuable to man. Found only in plants, chlorophyll appears to combat tumor growth, particularly in the lungs, by working on the adrenal glands and cleaning the lymph nodes, and enriching the blood and freeing clogged arteries. Try as we may, we cannot duplicate chlorophyll in the laboratory. But you can get sufficient chlorophyll in green leafy plants such as spinach and broccoli.

These are only a few of the ways juices made from fresh vegetables and fruits can enhance your life and help prevent a series of ailments, some deadly serious, others merely unpleasant. Beginning on page 152, I alphabetically list the fruits and vegetables I prefer for juicing. Read this section to learn about how to buy and store each item, and also to understand each one's special healthful benefits. Beginning on page 223 I describe the numerous health problems that are helped or sometimes prevented simply through a healthful diet of juice and raw fruits and vegetables. And perhaps most important, beginning on page 44, I have provided more than a hundred recipes for fresh, delicious fruit and vegetable juices that will ultimately benefit your good health.

And that is all there is to it—there are no tricks, no special formulas to buy, no foreign foods to seek out in weird shops, no pills, no powders to mix with water. I advocate eating foods easily found in every supermarket, farm stand, and greengrocer in the land.

Easy? Sensible? Delicious? You bet!

3

Setting Up a Natural Kitchen

*I*f you own a juicer, you are well on your way to outfitting your kitchen as a natural kitchen—a room where you will devise glorious juices and natural meals bursting with nutrition and good flavor. A natural kitchen is where good family health begins, where your children and friends will experience your love for them in the food you prepare and the juices you serve. A natural kitchen is a clean, light, friendly place—never smelling of cooking grease or overheated by sputtering skillets cooking the life out of food. There is not an unseemly abundance of overpackaged, overprocessed foods, sticky sugars, jams, jellies, or syrups in the cupboards or precooked food stuffed into plastic bags crammed in the freezer. Instead, the kitchen is stocked with fresh produce, fragrant herbs, and heady spices. The cupboards contain sacks of grains and beans and the refrigerator bulges with vegetables and fruits.

Whether yours is a tiny city apartment kitchen, a rambling country kitchen, or something in between, it can easily be stocked with the few items necessary for efficient juicing and natural cookery. Every time you enter the room, you will be met with the dazzling sight of baskets and bowls filled with colorful, fresh produce waiting to be juiced or otherwise consumed in their pure, natural state.

Organizing the Food in a Natural Kitchen

Regardless of how excited you are when you first bring home the juicer, if you do not follow a few easy rules for preparing and storing produce, your enthusiasm may wane before the benefits of juicing kick in.

Buy only as much as you will need for a week. Fresh produce spoils even under the best conditions, and it is distressful, not to mention wasteful, to toss rotten fruit and vegetables in the garbage or compost pile. Linda and I plan on twenty-five pounds of carrots a week for our family of four, and because carrots keep for a couple of weeks, we often buy them in fifty-pound sacks which we store in the garage refrigerator. We try to buy only organic produce—I will drive an hour out of my way for fifty pounds of organic carrots—

which we rinse with cold water and dry as soon as we get it home. Organically grown fruits and vegetables need nothing harsher than running cold water to rinse off any dirt that may have accumulated on them during picking and transporting.

If you cannot find organic fruits and vegetables, use a biodegradable produce wash to clean all produce. You can buy this product at your local health food store. Dry the produce with soft cloth towels or let it air-dry, then store it in the refrigerator or on the countertop, depending on the produce and its degree of ripeness (the guidelines for specific fruits and vegetables are in Chapter 5). Spin-dry greens, such as lettuce and spinach, and store them in the refrigerator in large, Ziploc plastic bags. Make sure the leaves are thoroughly dry, otherwise they may turn slimy in storage.

I cannot stress how important it is to clean all your produce as soon as you buy it. Nothing is more off-putting than having to wash and dry a bunch of spinach or parsley when the urge hits for a fresh glass of juice. In fact, you may shrug off the craving when faced with this task. If you take a little time after shopping to wash, dry, and store the produce, I promise that staying on the juice diet is effortless.

Buy herbs fresh if possible, or better yet, grow your own in windowsill pots or a small patch outside the kitchen door. If you use dried herbs and spices, keep them in glass bottles, if you can, and store them in a dark cupboard. Date the jars and bottles and discard any herbs and spices that are older than three or four months.

Grow your own sprouts (page 198) and wheatgrass (page 204). Sprouts are a terrific source of nutrition and could not be easier or less expensive to grow. Involve your children; they will get a kick out of this. Wheatgrass is a bit more of an undertaking than sprouts, but given wheatgrass's health benefits, it is worth it to make space for the growing trays in the pantry or corner of the kitchen.

Appliances and Equipment for a Natural Kitchen

While some appliances in the kitchen will become practically obsolete once you begin juicing, others will assume new significance. For instance, the microwave will collect dust but the refrigerator will become the focal point of kitchen activity. In fact, if your family is large, you might consider buying a second refrigerator for additional storage; you can often find a reliable secondhand one to keep in the basement or garage. If you are the sort of cook who rarely pays attention to knives and how sharp they are, you will now find yourself noting the edge on their blades and perhaps even purchasing a few new ones.

The juicer is the star of the natural kitchen. Give it a prominent place on the counter, preferably near the sink in an area with ample counter space. The whirrr of its motor will become a welcome sound in the house, enticing children and adults into the kitchen to sample the juice of the moment.

Here I will list the equipment I recommend for efficient and effortless healthful cookery and juicing. The needs are modest and you most likely already have most of what is required. First and foremost is the juicer. This is the only expensive item, but when you think how often you will use it in a day, a week, a month, its value is obvious. After all, you do not hesitate to spend money on a stove; to add juice to your life, the juicer is just as integral, if not more so—and it is far less costly.

The Juicer. The juicer I have is the greatest juicer available. During the more than forty years I have been lecturing and demonstrating how to juice, I have operated nearly three hundred different machines and none has changed my mind about the superiority of The Juiceman® juicer. But since more important than a juicer is the juice, I hope you will be inspired to buy a good juicer and start on the path to a healthier diet and a more vigorous life-style.

The difference between the price of juicers should be based on the size of the juicer's motor. A more expensive juicer should have at least a ⅝ horsepower electric motor capable of driving a tough, razor-sharp blade at 6,000 rpm. A less expensive juicer should still have a sturdy motor of at least ¼ horsepower. Together the motor and blade should be tough enough to handle skins, stems, and rinds in large quantities.

A juicer should be light, about ten pounds, and if it comes with a reinforced carrying case, all the better. This makes it easy to pack up and take with you on the road. I think this is important regardless of the kind of juicer you buy. The carrying case should be designed to fit easily in the overhead bins on airplanes and be light enough so you can carry it over your shoulder as you march through airports, train stations, or down busy avenues. This is especially important for me, as I travel all the time demonstrating the wonders of juicing—and can never be without a juicer right there in the hotel room so I can make the fresh juices I need for high energy and great health.

A juicer should be designed so that you can make juice after juice without disassembling and cleaning the machine every time. The basket should be slanted so that the moment food is put in the hopper, juices stream through the screen and the pulp slides up the wall and right out the back of the machine. The best blade basket is made of stainless steel and the pulp should collect outside the machine in a large receptacle—not inside the machine so that it has to be taken apart every time the pulp gets too bulky. If the pulp receptacle is free-standing it can be emptied without dismantling the machine. This sort of pulp receptacle is easy to clean too.

Other than the pulp receptacle and the machine base, there should be only a few other components to a juicer. The juice bowl, the screened blade basket, its housing, and the covering dome should fit together neatly and simply, snapping into place with a single mechanism that makes the juicer as easy to assemble as it is to take apart for cleaning. **Care and Cleaning of the Juicer:** As I mentioned, I suggest putting the juicer in a prominent place in the kitchen. Because you will be using a lot of vegetables and fruits that have to be washed and then cut into pieces, the ideal location is near a sink and on a counter with enough space for a large cutting board. Take care that the juicer's cord is not near the sink, and because some pulp and juice inevitably end up on the counter, store your cookbooks away from the juicer.

As you juice, pulp collects in the large receptacle. After eight to ten hours it develops a sour odor and tiny gnats and fruit flies may appear out of nowhere. I suggest emptying the pulp as often as possible. It makes marvelous compost but if you do not have a compost heap, toss it in the garbage. Many people (including myself) find it handy to line the receptacle with the plastic bags they collect from the supermarket when buying produce. This certainly makes emptying the pulp effortless—although plastic bags are not biodegradable, while the pulp is.

Clean the juicer after every use, otherwise the pulp will harden on the parts and make them slightly more difficult to clean. Depending on your schedule, clean the juicer once, twice, or more every day. Remember, I am not saying you have to clean it between juicing different types of juice: If you are making carrot juice and your spouse or child wants apple-pear juice, make both and then clean the juicer.

To clean the juicer, dismantle the removable parts and

rinse them under running water. If you have a spray attachment on the sink, it works well for this. There is no oil or sticky sugar that needs to be scrubbed away with detergent—clear water works just fine. The mesh screened basket usually requires a little scrubbing with a brush or soft, soap-free pad. Every few days I recommend soaking the parts in a two-to-one solution of dishwashing detergent (I use Shaklee automatic dishwashing concentrate Basic D) and chlorine bleach mixed into a sinkful of hot water. I use about a half cup of detergent and a quarter cup of bleach. If you leave the parts in this solution overnight, carrot and other stains will come right off with only a little rubbing. Be sure to rinse the parts thoroughly before re-assembling the juicer.

Other Equipment

Although the juicer is the most important piece of kitchen equipment for the juice diet, other items are also essential and still others are terribly helpful. I will list the equipment I find useful here in alphabetical order. Depending on your style of cooking and diet, you will find some more indispensable than others. I do not suggest anyone try to get along without knives and a cutting board.

Blender. A powerful blender is wonderful for making smoothies—juice combinations that cannot be accomplished solely with the juicer. For example, bananas are too soft to juice, but you can blend them with orange or pineapple juice to make a thick, delicious drink. You will also find yourself using the blender almost daily for salad dressings, soups, and sauces. I suggest buying a blender with a strong motor that will not lug down as it is used. Some also have detachable canisters that make storing blended food easy. Hand held blenders are great for salad dressings, soups and sauces—but not for blending juices.

A number of people over the years have asked me what the difference is between a juicer and a blender. Why can't they simply chop an apple up and blend it to make juice? The answer is simple: The blender purées or mashes fruit; the juicer releases the life-giving, body-building juice from the fruit or vegetable and discards the indigestible fiber. (The juice does retain a portion of soluble fiber.) Juice is absorbed into the body and its nutrients go to work almost immediately. Fiber takes hours to digest, and while it is a necessary part of everyone's diet, there are other ways to get it.

Cutting board. The best cutting boards I have found are made of white polyethelene plastic. These boards are easy to keep clean. Unlike wooden boards, they never warp, split, or develop mildew. I use one that is approximately 16 by 20 inches. When using this or any other cutting board, I lay a dish towel beneath it to prevent it from slipping on the counter as I work. I make sure the dish towel is smaller than the board—so it doesn't get soiled.

Food processor. Similar in function to a blender, food processors are generally more powerful and have more capacity. They are extremely useful for slicing large quantities of vegetables for vegetarian salads, and are great for making vegetable-based puréed soups, both cold and hot. I also like the manual Boerner slicer, called the V-slicer, which can perform many of the same tasks as a food processor.

Glass measure. Although not essential, it is extremely helpful to have a measuring glass with clearly marked ounce levels on its side. This enables you to see exactly how much juice a single fruit or vegetable yields, which is particularly important in the case of "green" juices that not only must be mixed with another juice, but that rarely should be taken in quantities of more than two or three ounces at one time.

Kitchen scale. A scale that weighs up to a pound is helpful when you are beginning to juice. (A five-pound scale is fine too.) How else will you know when you have a four-ounce bunch of grapes or ten ounces of cantaloupe? After a few weeks, you can put the scale away, as you will have learned how to "eyeball" the produce for the amount of juice you are making, though you may decide to keep it on the counter to weigh other foods such as grains and flour.

Knives. You may be surprised at the disparity in the cost of knives. If you think a knife is a knife, think again, and take my word for it, investing in a few high-quality knives is well worth it. They last a lifetime and make cutting and chopping a breeze. Made from alloyed, high-carbon stainless steel, good knives are well-balanced, sturdy tools that do not lose their cutting edges over time and, when dull, quickly regain their sharpness. Knives with hollowed blades—those with edges visibly hollowed from the blade—are not good bets. Price is generally a good indication of the quality of the knife. Also check that the tang of the blade extends all the way to the end of the handle, indicated in many knives by two or three rivets in the handle. Some knives have heavy-duty plastic handles without rivets. Finally, hold the knife in your hand. It should feel well balanced.

For most needs, a natural cook should have a couple of good paring knives with 3½-inch blades and an 8-inch chef's knife. A serrated bread knife is useful too. Keep the knives in a block or rack. Storing them in a drawer with other cutlery can cause them to dull as they bang against each other and you can inadvertently cut yourself reaching into the drawer.

While most knives nowadays are dishwasher-safe, I suggest washing them by hand as they will bump against other cutlery in the dishwasher, just as in the drawer, and this will spoil their edges.

A knife is only as good as its blade. Invest in a knife sharpener. (Do not confuse the honing steel with a sharpener. The steel is used to remove infinitesimal shards of metal from the knife blade between every use.) Sharpeners are either manual or electric and should be used as needed to keep the blade sharp. Most cooks judge sharpness by feel—how easily the knife slices through a tomato, for instance. As a general rule, knives need to be sharpened every two or three weeks.

Mini processor or coffee grinder. These little appliances are very useful for grinding small amounts of nuts and seeds. Both are equally effective. You can grind nuts and seeds in blenders and food processors, too, but the smaller appliances are quicker, easier to clean, and handle tiny quantities the best. However, you can also use a hand mill for grinding nuts and seeds.

Pots and pans. I suggest heavy-gauge stainless steel pots and pans. (Elderly people may find these too heavy to use and therefore should rely instead on lighter-weight stainless steel cookware.) I do not recommend aluminum pans under any conditions—traces of aluminum can leach out into food. For the same reason I urge you to stay away from nonstick pans. The coatings are made with aluminum-based chemicals and other toxins that have no business in your bloodstream. You will need several saucepans and a large pot for cooking pasta in rapidly boiling water. Make sure all your pots and pans have tight-fitting lids so that when you do cook food, as many nutrients as possible are trapped in the pan and do not escape with the steam.

Pressure cooker. I use the Fogacci pressure cooker and highly recommend it. When the pan is on the flame only the external base heats. This transmits heat to the water in the air space which in turn produces the steam that heats the internal wall of the container with the food. The control valve remains constantly at 105°C and even when the flame is raised, the temperature will not increase, ensuring that the food is cooked evenly. No more burned rice!

Salad spinner. These useful devices dry lettuce and other greens by centrifugal force. As the greens spin in the colander section of the spinner, they are not damaged at all and come out needing no further drying or just a little patting with a soft towel. I find spinners a great time-saver, particularly since Linda and I consume so many greens and lettuces during the course of a week.

Sprouting jars and lids. I suggest buying three 8- to 10-inch high sprouting jars for each of the most commonly used sprouts: alfalfa, adzuki, and peas/lentils (peas and lentils grow well together, so I list them as one). Each jar should have three different lids, easily purchased as a package in a health food store. One lid has tiny holes for the alfalfa sprouts and the other two have increasingly larger holes for the other sprouts.

Storage containers. Store greens, completely washed and dried, in large Ziploc plastic bags. These bags can be used over and over again and so are neither a great expense nor an environmental hazard. Some Tupperware is great for storing washed and dried greens too. Otherwise, I like to use glass rather than plastic for storage because glass doesn't pick up odors and over time some plastics may give off harmful chemicals. I do, though, use glass containers with plastic lids. Never store food in metal containers and most definitely not in aluminum. For preparing and serving food, I recommend glass or stoneware dishes and bowls and wooden utensils for serving.

Strainers. I usually strain the juice as it comes from the juicer, although many people prefer it just as it is. Try to find strainers with fine meshes that are not made completely of steel. I like those made by Cuisine Queen. About once a month when they discolor from carrots, I soak the strainers in a sink of scalding water mixed with a cup of dishwashing liquid. Then they look as good as new.

Vegetable brush. Buy a sturdy vegetable brush to use on tough-skinned produce such as potatoes and carrots. This is particularly important for organically grown fruits and vegetables, which, although pesticide-free, may have some honest garden dirt clinging to them. The brush also comes in handy for cleaning the juicer's mesh-screened basket.

These few utensils and appliances will make the juice diet easy and pleasurable. I urge you to arrange your work space so that everything is easy to reach—no need for clumsy maneuvering to pull a mixing bowl or blender canister from the back of the closet. Clean out drawers and cupboards; reorganize the refrigerator; buy some handsome baskets and bowls to hold fruits and vegetables for easy access to them and also to keep them in plain view so you can enjoy their pretty colors and shapes. And children automatically gravitate to these types of food when they are out on display. I promise, the sounds of the knife chopping and the juicer juicing are sure to become the best parts of your day.

4

The Recipes

The recipes are the heart and soul of this book. And like anything with a lot of heart, they are generous, forgiving, and flexible. In other words, use the combinations of fruits and vegetables that follow to make delectable, frothy juices, and then, when you are ready, experiment on your own with similar combinations. For example, if you have a whole pint of strawberries and a pineapple but no apples, juice what you have. Don't worry that you cannot make the juice I call Tropical Sunset. Devise your own delicious drink. If you have only three carrots and the recipe says to use four, make the juice anyway. Or perhaps the idea of juicing blueberries with kiwi and apples appeals to you. Why not? Try it.

Green Juices

The exception to this "anything goes" philosophy is "green" vegetable juice. Always, always, always mix green juices with a more palatable and milder juice such as carrot or apple, otherwise you may experience temporary gastric discomfort. Green juices are made from nearly anything green: spinach, broccoli, kale, lettuce, wheatgrass, parsley. Celery and cucumbers are exceptions. Only a quarter of the glass should be filled with green juice. The rest must be carrot or apple, or sometimes celery. Also, do not drink more than four ounces of beet or two ounces of wheatgrass juice at one time.

To juice leafy vegetables such as lettuce, parsley, spinach, and greens, bunch the leaves between your fingers and push them into the hopper, using the plunger to push them all the way into the juicer. To juice sprouts, wrap them in a lettuce or cabbage leaf and push the whole packet into the juicer. When juicing soft foods such as berries, pears, and greens, it's a good idea to juice the firm fruits or vegetables, such as carrots and apples, first and last. That way the softer food will not clog the juicer as the firmer produce flushes it out. Use apples to "clean" the juicer between different juice recipes. This is not a substitute for washing the juicer with water after using it, but this does eliminate the necessity of doing it when making a variety of different juices at one time.

Fruits and Vegetables
Do Not Mix

Remember that fruit and vegetable juices do not mix. The two primary exceptions to this are carrots and apples. I have organized the recipes so that those under "Vegetable Juices," however, may sometimes contain apple (even cantaloupe, pear, and pineapple too).

Drink the juices right away. They are not meant to be made, poured into a container, and stored for later consumption. Soon after juicing, nutrients begin to lose their power, and so to enjoy the full benefits of the juice, drink it immediately after it flows from the juicer. And if you are drinking vegetable juice, be sure to "chew" it. This means swirling it around in your mouth until it feels warm and tastes sweet. This motion and the food activate the naturally occurring digestive enzymes in the saliva.

Getting Ready to Juice

Because it is important to drink juices directly after juicing, I suggest here and in other places in the book that you wash the produce as soon as you get home from the market and then store it properly so it is ready to juice when you are ready to juice it. Unless it is organically grown, be sure to use a gentle, biodegradable natural cleanser to rid the food of harmful pesticide and other chemical residue. (See Chapter 3, "Setting Up a Natural Kitchen," and Chapter 5, "Fruits and Vegetables—and Why They Are So Good for You," for more information on buying, washing, and storing fruits and vegetables.)

Fruit Juices

Fruit juices are energizers and body cleansers. I drink at least two glasses every day.

Remember to wash and scrub all produce well. Read Chapter 5 for information on how to prepare specific fruits for juicing. Be especially careful about pineapple skin and melon rind. If the fruits are not organic, do not juice the rind or skin.

Anti-Virus Cocktail

Apple-Orange Juice

One serving about 8 ounces

This is the drink of choice in our house before school in the wintertime. The boys never complain! Simple? Sure. But you don't mess with a classic. This is one of the all-time great fruit juices.

2 apples

1 orange

Cut the apples into narrow wedges. Peel the orange, leaving on as much white pith as possible. Cut or break the orange into segments. Process the fruit in the juicer.

Apricot Ambrosia
Apricot-Grape-Pear Juice

One serving about 8 ounces

This combination makes a summer drink to remember, especially if you use red grapes.

4 apricots

1 (3-ounce) bunch of green or red grapes, preferably organic, with stems

1 pear

Cut the apricots in half and remove the pits, then cut them into narrow wedges. If the grapes are not organic, remove the stems. Cut the pear into narrow wedges. Process the fruit in the juicer.

The Arouser
Grape-Cherry Juice

One serving about 8 ounces

I love this juice in the summertime over ice. As for the name. Well, it does the trick every time. And you know what—some people have told me it helps them ward off cavities too! Try adding a little apple juice for more complex flavor.

2 (4-ounce) bunches of black grapes, organic if possible, with stems

1/2 cup black cherries, pitted

If the grapes are not organic, remove the stems. Process the fruit in the juicer.

Bromelain Plus
Pineapple Juice

One serving about 8 ounces

This is the drink to take away my aches and pains. I'd be lost without it. Pineapple is a traditional symbol of hospitality. So whenever you have guests, serve them Bromelain Plus!

2 (1-inch-thick) pineapple rounds, preferably organic

If the pineapple is not organic, remove and discard the skin. Cut the rounds into strips. Process the pineapple strips, including the core, in the juicer.

Cantaloupe Juice

One serving about 8 ounces

I think this juice is sensational. It supplies the body with lots of beta carotene; we drink it in the summer for its great taste and because it helps digestion.

About 12 ounces of cantaloupe (approximately 1/4 cantaloupe)

Cut the cantaloupe into strips. Process the melon, rind and all, in the juicer.

The Cape Codder
Apple-Cranberry Juice

One serving about 8 ounces

I drink this all winter long. The sweetness of the apples cuts the tartness of the berries—what could be better? You can taste the brisk sea air of Cape Cod with every sip. And you will never drink bottled cranberry juice again.

3 apples

1 cup cranberries

Cut the apple into narrow wedges. Process the fruit in the juicer.

Christmas Cocktail
Apple-Grape-Lemon Juice

One serving about 8 ounces

I developed this recipe more than twenty-five years ago and still find it the best party punch for the holidays.

3 Golden Delicious or other sweet apples

1 (4-ounce) bunch of green or purple grapes, preferably organic, with stems

¼ lemon, with the skin

Cut the apples into narrow wedges. If the grapes are not organic, remove the stems. Cut the lemon into slices. Process the apple wedges and grapes in the juicer, adding the lemon slices about halfway through.

Cranberry-Grape-Pineapple Juice

One serving about 8 ounces

For fresh flavor in the dead of winter, try this. I don't know exactly why, but this drink just makes me smile.

1 cup cranberries

1 (4-ounce) bunch of green grapes, preferably organic, with stems

1 (1-inch-thick) pineapple round, preferably organic

If the grapes are not organic, remove the stems. If the pineapple is not organic, remove and discard the skin. Cut the round into strips. Process the fruit in the juicer.

Dawn Patrol
Orange Juice

One serving about 8 ounces

*O*range juice as you have never experienced it before—creamy, smooth, and rich. You haven't had orange juice until you've had this drink.

2 to 3 oranges

Peel the oranges, leaving on as much white pith as possible. Cut or break the oranges into segments. Process the fruit in the juicer.

Digestive Cocktail

Orange-Grapefruit-Lemon Juice
(alkaline drink)

One serving about 8 ounces

This is terrific after a tough workout—or a big meal!

1 orange

1/4 grapefruit

1/4 lemon, with the skin

Peel the orange and the grapefruit, leaving on as much white pith as possible. Cut or break the fruit into segments, and slice the lemon. Process the fruit in the juicer.

57

Evening Regulator
Apple-Pear Juice

One serving about 8 ounces

We love to drink this soothing juice before going to sleep.

2 to 3 apples

1 pear

Cut the apples and pear into narrow wedges. Beginning and ending with a few apple wedges, process the fruit in the juicer.

Eve's Promise
Apple-Pomegranate Juice

One serving about 8 ounces

Our children are crazy about this! Peeling and juicing the pomegranate is like a game for them. Pomegranate is a good source of vitamin C and potassium.

2 Golden Delicious or other sweet apples

½ pomegranate

Cut the apples into narrow wedges. Peel the pomegranate and cut it into narrow wedges. Process the fruit in the juicer.

Note: If you find this juice to be too bitter, separate the pomegranate seeds and juice just the seeds with the wedges of apple.

The Eye-Opener
Grapefruit Juice

One serving about 8 ounces

This will leave you with a special tingle. Remember, heavy grapefruits have more juice.

1 grapefruit

Peel the grapefruit, leaving on as much white pith as possible. Cut or separate it into segments. Process the fruit in the juicer.

Fruit Cocktail
Orange-Lime Juice

One serving about 8 ounces

If the day is warm, throw this juice into your blender with ice cubes for a dazzling, fizzy, frozen drink.

1 orange

½ lime, with the skin

½ cup sparkling mineral water, chilled

Orange slice for garnish

Peel the orange, leaving on as much white pith as possible. Cut or break the orange into segments. Cut the lime into slices. Process the fruit in the juicer. Add the mineral water and garnish with the orange slice.

The Juiceman's Power of Juicing

Fruit Cooler
Orange-Lime Juice

One serving about 8 ounces

7 his is a super vitamin C combination and as such a great wintertime drink to help ward off colds.

1 large orange

½ lime, with the skin

¼ cups sparkling mineral water

Orange slice for garnish

Peel the orange, leaving on as much white pith as possible. Cut or break the orange into segments. Cut the lime into slices. Process the fruit in the juicer. Add the mineral water and garnish with the orange slice.

Georgia Peach Cooler
Peach-Orange Juice

One serving about 8 ounces

It's the peaches that give this juice its unbelievable flavor. If Georgia's on your mind, grab a glass of this delectable cooler. Peaches are at their best in the summer. They are a good source of provitamin A, potassium, and magnesium. Firm peaches juice better than overripe peaches.

1 peach

1 orange

¼ cup sparkling mineral water

2 slices of lime for garnish

Cut the peach into narrow wedges. Discard the pit. Peel the orange, leaving on as much white pith as possible. Cut or break the orange into segments. Process the fruit in the juicer. Add the mineral water and garnish with the lime slices.

Ginger Jolt
Apple-Pear-Ginger Juice

One serving about 8 ounces

We serve this drink to friends—it tastes good and tickles your nose! And many people have told me that a glass of this before a bumpy plane trip or a choppy ocean voyage helps stave off queasiness.

2 apples

1 pear

1-inch knob of gingerroot

Cut the apples and pear into narrow wedges. Slice the gingerroot if necessary. Beginning and ending with apple, process half the apple and pear wedges in the juicer. Process the ginger. Process the remaining apple and pear wedges, beginning and ending with apple.

Grape-Pineapple Punch

One serving about 8 ounces

Try using black Ribeir grapes in this punch. Linda and I make it often in the fall.

1 (4-ounce) bunch of green grapes, preferably organic, with stems

1 (1-inch-thick) pineapple round, preferably organic

½ lemon, with the skin

Handful of seedless green grapes for garnish

or

½ cup pineapple chunks for garnish

or

1 strip lemon zest for garnish

If the grapes are not organic, remove the stems. If the pineapple is not organic, remove and discard the skin. Cut the round into strips. Cut the lemon into slices. Process the fruit in the juicer. Garnish with additional grapes, pineapple chunks, or the twist of lemon zest.

The Juiceman's Power of Juicing

Honeydew-Lime Juice

One serving about 8 ounces

*F*or a thirst quencher, this is better than tonic and lime by a long shot. Sweet and tart—it's like drinking a candy.

About 12 ounces of honeydew melon (approximately ¼ honeydew)

¼ lime, with the skin

Cut the honeydew into strips. Cut the lime into slices. Process the melon rind and all, and the lime in the juicer.

Honolulu-California Connector

Pineapple-Strawberry Juice

One serving about 8 ounces

I consider this tropical nectar delicious anytime.

1 (1-inch-thick) pineapple round,
    preferably organic

8 strawberries

If the pineapple is not organic, remove and discard the skin. Cut the round into strips. Process the fruit in the juicer.

Jay's World Famous Lemonade
Apple-Lemon Juice

One serving about 8 ounces

W hat can I say? This is simply the best-tasting drink you can make.

4 apples

1/4 lemon, with the skin

Crushed ice

Cut the apples into narrow wedges, and slice the lemon. Process the fruit in the juicer. Serve over crushed ice.

The Key Wester
Grapefruit-Pineapple-Apple-Lime Juice
(calcium drink)

One serving about 8 ounces

After a long tour lecturing and appearing on televison, I like to come home, make a tall glass of this juice, and relax in the sun. When you use Key Limes from Florida, the taste is out of this world.

¼ grapefruit

1 (1-inch-thick) pineapple round, preferably organic

1 apple

1 small slice of lime

Peel the grapefruit, leaving on as much white pith as possible. Cut or break the grapefruit into segments. If the pineapple is not organic, remove and discard the skin. Cut the round into strips. Cut the apple into narrow wedges. Process the fruit in the juicer.

The Juiceman's Power of Juicing

69

Kiwi Kick
Grape-Kiwi-Orange Juice

One serving about 8 ounces

The flavors play off one another deliciously—and you get a burst of energy!

1 (4-ounce) bunch of green grapes, preferably organic, with stems

3 kiwis

1 Valencia orange

If the grapes are not organic, remove the stems. Cut the kiwis into narrow wedges. Peel the orange, leaving on as much white pith as possible, and cut or break it into segments. Process the fruit in the juicer.

Linda's Morning Sunrise
Grapefruit-Orange-Strawberry Juice

One serving about 8 ounces

The news in the paper may be bad and the weather awful—but this delicious drink starts every day off on a great note.

¼ pink grapefruit

1 orange

6 to 8 strawberries

Peel the grapefruit and the orange, leaving on as much white pith as possible. Cut or break the grapefruit and orange into segments. Process the fruit in the juicer.

The Juiceman's Power of Juicing

71

Mango-Lemon Cooler

One serving about 8 ounces

My older son, John, calls this his "happy drink."

1 mango

¼ lemon, with the skin

½ cup sparkling mineral water

Crushed ice

Lemon slice for garnish

Remove the skin from the mango. Cut the mango in half and remove the pit. Cut each half into strips. Cut the lemon into slices. Process the mango strips and lemon slices in the juicer. Add the mineral water and crushed ice. Garnish with the slice of lemon.

Miami Cool
Pineapple-Orange Juice

One serving about 8 ounces

The fresh taste of Florida fruit starts the day right. Try it over ice when the temperature rises. The drink also has great "Art Deco" color. The next best thing to a trip to the Fontainebleau Hotel.

1 (1-inch-thick) pineapple round, preferably organic

1 orange

If the pineapple is not organic, remove and discard the skin. Cut the round into strips. Peel the orange, leaving on as much white pith as possible. Cut or break the orange into segments. Process the fruit in the juicer.

Morning Blush
Pineapple-Grapefruit Juice

One serving about 8 ounces

My favorite: sweet and sour for breakfast.

1 (1-inch thick) pineapple round, preferably organic

½ pink grapefruit

If the pineapple is not organic, remove and discard the skin. Cut the round into strips. Peel the grapefruit, leaving on as much white pith as possible. Cut or break the grapefruit into segments. Process the fruit in the juicer.

New England Charmer
Apple-Cranberry-Grape Juice

One serving about 8 ounces

The sweetness of grapes turns this classic into a surefire winner, perfect for sipping on a big screened porch while surveying the fine New England summertime countryside.

2 apples

1 cup cranberries

1 (4-ounce) bunch of green or red grapes, preferably organic

Cut the apples into narrow wedges. If the grapes are not organic, remove the stems. Process the fruit in the juicer.

New Zealand Zinger
Apple-Kiwi Juice

One serving about 8 ounces

You'll love this. The kiwi tastes a little like strawberries and makes this just a bit different from other juices.

2 *Golden Delicious or other sweet apples*

4 *kiwis*

Cut the apples and kiwis into narrow wedges. Process the fruit in the juicer.

Party-Time Cocktail
Pineapple-Orange-Lemon Juice

One serving about 8 ounces

Our children and their friends especially like this one. We seem to make it often on Saturday afternoons when the boys invite friends over to play. But it's not just for kids—adults love it too.

1 (1-inch-thick) pineapple round, preferably organic

1 orange

½ lemon, with the skin

If the pineapple is not organic, remove and discard the skin. Cut the round into strips. Peel the orange, leaving on as much white pith as possible. Cut or break the orange into segments. Cut the lemon into slices. Process the fruit in the juicer.

Passion Cocktail
Pineapple-Grape-Strawberry Juice

One serving about 8 ounces

L inda and I sip this as we watch the sun going down over the Nevada desert.

1 (1-inch-thick) pineapple round,
    preferably organic

1 (4-ounce) bunch of green grapes,
    preferably organic, with stems

6 strawberries

If the pineapple is not organic, remove and discard the skin. Cut the rounds into strips. If the grapes are not organic, remove the stems. Process the fruit in the juicer.

Pear-Apple Cocktail

One serving about 8 ounces

I have enjoyed this juice for more than thirty years. Pears rank among my very favorite fruits for juicing and eating.

2 pears

1 apple

¼ lemon, with the skin

Edible flowers for garnish (optional)

Crushed ice (optional)

Cut the pears and apple into narrow wedges. Cut the lemon into slices. Process the fruit in the juicer. Garnish with the flowers and serve over crushed ice, if desired.

The Juiceman's Power of Juicing

79

Persimmon-Orange Juice

One serving about 8 ounces

7 ry this; it's zingy and great! The persimmons sold in most markets are Japanese fruit—not the small native fruit that fall from persimmon trees predominantly in the Midwest. Be sure the large, bright orange, slightly elongated fruit are ripe, otherwise their high tannin content will leave them bitter. Persimmons are a source of Vitamin C, potassium, magnesium, and provitamin A.

1 persimmon

1 orange

Peel the persimmon and the orange, leaving on as much white pith as possible. Cut the persimmon into narrow wedges, and cut or break the orange into segments. Process the fruit in the juicer.

Pineapple-Cherry Smasher
Pineapple-Lime-Cherry Juice

One serving about 8 ounces

The color of this juice is beautiful, but you will also appreciate the energy boost and great flavor.

2 (1-inch-thick) pineapple rounds, preferably organic

1 lime, with the skin

2 to 3 whole, pitted cherries for garnish

½ cup pineapple chunks for garnish

If the pineapple is not organic, remove and discard the skin. Cut the rounds into strips. Cut the lime into narrow wedges. Process the lime wedges and pineapple strips in the juicer. Add the pineapple chunks and the cherries for garnish.

Pink Flush
Pink Grapefruit-Apple Juice

One serving about 8 ounces

Trying to lose a little weight? Drink this to satisfy hunger pangs between meals.

½ pink grapefruit

2 apples

Peel the grapefruit, leaving on as much white pith as possible. Cut or break the grapefruit into segments. Cut the apple into narrow wedges. Process the fruit in the juicer.

Rosy Richee
Orange-Pineapple-Raspberry Juice
(alkaline drink)

One serving about 8 ounces

I love fresh raspberries, both to eat and to juice—in my book they are the crème de la crème of all berries.

1 orange

1 (1-inch-thick) pineapple round, preferably organic

½ cup raspberries

Peel the orange, leaving on as much white pith as possible. Cut or break the orange into segments. If the pineapple is not organic, remove and discard the skin. Cut the round into strips. Process the fruit in the juicer.

San Francisco Fog Cutter
Apple-Strawberry Juice

One serving about 8 ounces

What a wonderful color this juice is, and I love the taste. Plus, it is a great blood purifier.

3 Golden Delicious or other sweet apples

8 strawberries

Cut the apples into narrow wedges. Process the fruit in the juicer.

Singing Apple Juice
Apple-Ginger Juice

One serving about 8 ounces

The zing of ginger makes apple juice sing a jaunty tune.

4 apples

1-inch knob of gingerroot

Cut the apples into narrow wedges. Cut the gingerroot into slices. Process the apples wedges and ginger slices in the juicer.

Strawberry-Grape Juice

One serving about 8 ounces

Linda drinks this juice to keep her complexion radiant.

8 strawberries
2 (4-ounce) bunches of green or purple grapes, preferably organic, with stems

If the grapes are not organic, remove the stems. Process the fruit in the juicer.

Summer Cooler
Orange-Lime-Peach Juice

One serving about 8 ounces

The fizzing mineral water and sweet taste make this a good introductory juice for kids who may be used to drinking soda. Fuzzy, rosy peaches are at their very best in the summer. They are rich in provitamin A, potassium, and magnesium. Firm peaches juice better than very ripe ones. But the riper the peach, the more delicious it is for eating.

1 orange

½ lime, with the skin

1 peach

¼ cup sparkling mineral water

Crushed ice (optional)

Peel the orange, leaving on as much white pith as possible. Cut or break the orange into segments. Cut the lime into slices. Cut the peach into narrow wedges, and discard the pit. Process the fruit in the juicer. Add the mineral water and serve over crushed ice, if desired.

The Juiceman's Power of Juicing

Tangerine Sky
Tangerine-Pineapple-Grape Juice
(calcium drink)

One serving about 8 ounces

*F*antastic in the wintertime, this is the perfect juice for an afternoon "pick-me-up."

2 medium or 3 small tangerines

1 (1-inch-thick) pineapple round, preferably organic

1 (3-ounce) bunch of red grapes, preferably organic, with stems

Peel the tangerines, leaving on as much white pith as possible. Cut or break the tangerines into segments. If the pineapple is not organic, remove and discard the skin. Cut the round into strips. If the grapes are not organic, remove the stems. Process the fruit in the juicer.

Triple P Juice
Persimmon-Pineapple-Pear Juice

One serving about 8 ounces

The three p's add up to just about perfect. The tastes go together so well it is unbelievable. Give your friends a glass and see if they can guess what fruits are in this juice. (Persimmons are a good source of vitamin C, provitamin A, potassium, and magnesium. This is a very healthy drink!)

1 persimmon

1 (½-inch-thick) pineapple round, preferably organic

1 pear

Peel the persimmon and cut it into narrow wedges. If the pineapple is not organic, remove and discard the skin. Cut the round into strips. Cut the pear into narrow wedges. Process the fruit in the juicer.

Tropical Nectar

Pineapple-Passion Fruit-Papaya-Nectarine Juice

One serving about 8 ounces

One sip of this and you will swear you are in the islands. The juice from the flesh inside the bumpy, stiff, dark purple-brown passion fruit shell is indescribably sweet and fragrant. These fruit travel well. And the nectarine juice is delicious. Nectarines are an ancient fruit (not a cross between a peach and a plum!) and have a good supply of provitamin A and potassium.

1 (1-inch-thick) pineapple round, preferably organic

1 passion fruit

1 small or ½ large papaya

1 small nectarine

If the pineapple is not organic, remove and discard the skin. Cut the round into strips. Cut the passion fruit into narrow wedges. Cut the papaya and nectarine into narrow wedges. Process the fruit in the juicer.

Tropical Sunset

Pineapple-Apple-Strawberry Juice

One serving about 8 ounces

*T*his is my younger son, Jayson's favorite.

1 (1-inch-thick) pineapple round, preferably organic

1 Red Delicious or other sweet apple

6 strawberries

If the pineapple is not organic, remove and discard the skin. Cut the round into strips. Cut the apple into narrow wedges. Process the fruit in the juicer.

Watermelon Juice

One serving about 8 ounces

*T*his is a terrific summer cooler that I drink all day long—particularly when the desert sun seems almost too hot.

About 10 ounces of watermelon (approximately ⅛ watermelon)

Cut the watermelon into strips. Process the melon, rind and all, in the juicer.

Winter's Foe

Pineapple-Tangerine Juice

One serving about 8 ounces

For vitamin C in the winter, Winter's Foe is one of your best choices. When your office mates start to sniffle, fortify yourself with this delicious juice.

1 (1-inch-thick) pineapple round, preferably organic

3 to 4 tangerines

If the pineapple is not organic, remove and discard the skin. Cut the round into strips. Peel the tangerines, leaving on as much white pith as possible. Cut or break the tangerines into segments. Process the fruit in the juicer.

Vegetable Juices

Vegetable juices are the building blocks, supplying the body with necessary vitamins and minerals to build strong bones and tissue. I drink at least four glasses a day.

If you find that some of these juice combinations are too strong for you, try diluting them with at least 25 percent water for your first months of juicing.

Be sure to read Chapter 5 for information on how to prepare different vegetables for juicing—and to find out all the glorious things vegetables can do for your body. And make sure to wash all vegetables.

Some of these juices also use fruit—but the emphasis in these recipes is on the wonderful, life-giving nutrients that come from the vegetable ingredients.

AAA Juice

Carrot-Celery-Apple-Beet-Wheatgrass-Parsley

One serving about 8 ounces

You cannot beat this juice for keeping your immune system healthy, which explains its triple-A rating.

3 carrots

1 stalk of celery

1 apple

½ beet with the greens

½ handful of wheatgrass

½ handful of parsley

Trim the carrots and cut them into 2- to 3-inch pieces. Cut the celery into 2- to 3-inch pieces. Cut the apple and beet into narrow wedges. Beginning and ending with the carrot and celery pieces, process the vegetables and apple wedges in the juicer.

The Juiceman's Power of Juicing

Alkaline Special
Carrot-Cabbage-Celery Juice

One serving about 8 ounces

This soothing drink will balance your system if it is too acidic or you feel gassy.

2 carrots

1 (3-inch) wedge of red or green cabbage

4 stalks of celery

Trim the carrots and cut them into 2- to 3-inch pieces. Cut the cabbage into narrow wedges. Cut the celery into 2- to 3-inch pieces. Process the vegetables in the juicer.

Anti-Ulcer Cabbage Cocktail

Tomato-Cabbage-Celery Juice

One serving about 8 ounces

This juice may soothe your stomach and calm your frazzled nerves. When the going gets tough, head for the juicer.

½ tomato

1 (4-inch) wedge of green cabbage

2 stalks of celery

Cut the tomato into narrow wedges. Cut the cabbage into narrow wedges. Cut the celery into 2- to 3-inch pieces. Process the vegetables in the juicer.

The Blemish Blaster
Carrot-Green Bell Pepper Juice

One serving about 8 ounces

*I*f your skin is not as clear as you would like, drink this for good epidermal health. It goes without saying that teenagers will want to drink a lot of this.

6 carrots

½ green bell pepper

Trim the carrots and cut them into 2- to 3-inch pieces. Cut the pepper into strips. Process the vegetables in the juicer.

Blood Regenerator
Carrot-Spinach-Lettuce-Turnip-Parsley Juice

One serving about 8 ounces

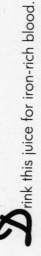

Drink this juice for iron-rich blood.

5 carrots

6 spinach leaves

4 lettuce leaves

¼ turnip

4 sprigs of parsley

Trim the carrots and cut them into 2- to 3-inch pieces. Process the vegetables in the juicer.

Body Cleanser
Carrot-Cucumber-Beet Juice

One serving about 8 ounces

I drink this to flush toxins from my system—and because it tastes so good. Remember, it is essential to mix beet juice with milder juices. If you eat a lot of meat, drink this juice!

2 to 3 carrots

½ cucumber

½ beet with the greens

Trim the carrots and cut them into 2- to 3-inch pieces. Cut the cucumber into quarters and cut the quarters into strips. Cut the beet into narrow wedges. Process the vegetables in the juicer.

Note: You can substitute ½ of a small zucchini for the cucumber to make a different, delicious cleansing cocktail.

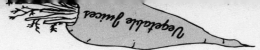

Bone-Building Tonic
Carrot-Kale-Parsley-Apple Juice

One serving about 8 ounces

Strong bones are essential to overall good health. Our kids like this combination. Yours will too.

5 to 6 carrots

4 kale leaves

4 sprigs of parsley

½ apple

Trim the carrots and cut them into 2- to 3-inch pieces. Cut the apple into narrow wedges. Process the vegetables and the apple wedges in the juicer.

Brittle Nails Juice
Carrot-Parsnip Juice

One serving about 8 ounces

*A*re your nails brittle and chipped? Drink this juice regularly and watch the problem disappear. It's so good, though, you will want to add it to your regular juice list.

6 carrots

½ parsnip

Trim the carrots and cut them into 2- to 3-inch pieces. Cut the parsnip into strips. Process the vegetables in the juicer.

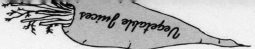

The Broccoli Cheer
Carrot-Broccoli-Apple Juice

One serving about 8 ounces

Try serving this juice to your children if they don't seem to like vegetables. They'll never know it's good for them. Tell them when they are older.

4 carrots

3 to 4 broccoli florets with stems

½ apple

Trim the carrots and cut them into 2- to 3-inch pieces. Slice the broccoli florets and stems into strips, if necessary. Cut the apple into narrow wedges. Process the vegetables and apple wedges in the juicer.

The Bunny Hop

Carrot-Spinach-Turnip Leaves-Watercress Juice

One serving about 8 ounces

This "rabbit food" juice provides you with so many nu-trients you will feel powerful enough to take on Mr. McGregor.

5 carrots

10 spinach leaves

4 turnip leaves

4 sprigs of watercress

Trim the carrots and cut them into 2- to 3-inch pieces. Process the vegetables in the juicer.

The Bushwacker
Carrot-Broccoli Juice

One serving about 8 ounces

The beta carotene makes this so good for you—and it tastes so delicious too—we think the President might even enjoy a swallow or two.

6 carrots

3 broccoli florets with stems

Trim the carrots and cut them into 2- to 3-inch pieces. Slice the broccoli florets and stems into strips, if necessary. Process the vegetables in the juicer.

Calming Nightcap
Carrot-Celery-Parsley Juice

One serving about 8 ounces

This will carry you off to the land of nod in a wink. There is no more natural sleep aid—unless you count counting sheep.

5 carrots

2 stalks of celery

Large handful of parsley

Trim the carrots and cut them into 2- to 3-inch pieces. Cut the celery into 2- to 3-inch pieces. Process the vegetables in the juicer.

Carrot-Beet Juice

One serving about 8 ounces

This has become a family favorite in our Las Vegas home. The color is like the most beautiful sunset. It is wonderful for you. What more can I say?

6 carrots

½ beet with the greens

Trim the carrots and cut them into 2- to 3-inch pieces. Cut the beet into narrow wedges. Beginning and ending with the carrot pieces, process the vegetables in the juicer.

The Juiceman's Power of Juicing

Carrot-Cabbage Juice
(alkaline drink)

One serving about 8 ounces

I find this juice energizing and calming, both at the same time. Drink it after a long, hectic day when you need to relax your nerves—but still have a busy night ahead.

4 to 5 carrots

1 (4-inch) wedge of green cabbage

Trim the carrots and cut them into 2- to 3-inch pieces. Cut the cabbage into narrow wedges. Process the vegetables in the juicer.

Carrot-Cantaloupe Cooler

One serving about 8 ounces

I love this combination. It's low in calories, has lots of beta carotene, and does wonders for the complexion.

4 carrots

About 6 ounces of cantaloupe (approximately 1/8 cantaloupe)

Trim the carrots and cut them into 2- to 3-inch pieces. Cut the cataloupe into strips. Process the carrot pieces and melon, rind and all, in the juicer.

Carrot-Cauliflower-Apple-Parsley Juice

One serving about 8 ounces

7 he sweet apple makes this vegetable juice particularly appealing.

4 carrots

2 cauliflower florets with stems

1 Golden Delicious or other sweet apple

Handful of parsley

Trim the carrots and cut them into 2- to 3-inch pieces. Slice the cauliflower florets and stems into strips, if necessary. Cut the apple into narrow wedges. Process the vegetables and apple wedges in the juicer.

Carrot-Cucumber Juice
(alkaline drink)

One serving about 8 ounces

This is as soothing as Carrot-Cabbage Juice but has the added benefit of being naturally cooling because of the cucumber. Try some after a long, hectic, hot day.

4 carrots

½ cucumber

Trim the carrots and cut them into 2- to 3-inch pieces. Cut the cucumber into quarters and cut the quarters into strips. Process the vegetables in the juicer.

The Carrot Top
Carrot-Beet Juice
(calcium drink)

One serving about 8 ounces

This brightly colored juice is tops for nutrition.

4 carrots

1 beet with the greens

Trim the carrots and cut them into 2- to 3-inch pieces. Cut the beet into narrow wedges. Process the vegetables in the juicer.

Cauliflower Quaff
Cauliflower-Carrot-Parsley Juice

One serving about 8 ounces

Cauliflower is a good source of potassium and phosphorus. Be sure to mix it with carrot juice, as I do here, to make it easy to digest.

4 to 5 cauliflower florets with stems

4 carrots

Handful of parsley

Slice the cauliflower florets and stems, if necessary. Trim the carrots and cut them into 2- to 3-inch lengths. Process the vegetables in the juicer.

The Champ
Carrot-Apple Juice

One serving about 8 ounces

7 his has been my favorite for more than forty years. I believe it saved my life.

4 carrots

2 apples

Trim the carrots and cut them into 2- to 3-inch pieces. Cut the apples into narrow wedges. Process the carrot pieces and apple wedges in the juicer.

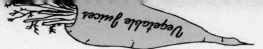

Chicago Winter Tonic
Carrot-Beet-Parsley Juice

One serving about 8 ounces

For vigor, for health, for looking and feeling great, here is a fabulous drink. Chicago is a high-energy town—and this is a high-energy juice.

6 carrots

½ beet with the greens

3 sprigs of parsley

Trim the carrots and cut them into 2- to 3-inch pieces. Cut the beet into narrow wedges. Process the vegetables in the juicer.

Cholesterol-Lowering Cocktail

Carrot-Apple-Ginger-Parsley Juice

One serving about 8 ounces

Drinking fresh juices low in calories and devoid of saturated fat is a good way to get your cholesterol levels down.

5 carrots

½ apple

½-inch knob of gingerroot

Handful of parsley

Trim the carrots and cut them into 2- to 3-inch pieces. Cut the apple into narrow wedges. Slice the gingerroot, if necessary. Process the carrot pieces, apple wedges, ginger, and parsley in the juicer.

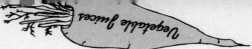
Vegetable Juices

Crimson Song

Carrot-Beet-Lettuce-Swiss Chard Juice
(alkaline drink)

One serving about 8 ounces

We make this drink for our sons when we feel they have not had enough raw salad. Of course, we also make sure they get plenty of fiber.

4 carrots

1 beet with the greens

7 to 8 lettuce leaves

or

2 to 4 Swiss chard leaves

Trim the carrots and cut them into 2- to 3-inch pieces. Cut the beet into narrow wedges. Process the vegetables in the juicer.

Digestive Special
Carrot-Spinach Juice
(alkaline drink)

One serving about 8 ounces

*I*t helps with digestion and is packed with vitamins. Powerful stuff! I recommend you sip this with your meal.

6 to 7 carrots

Handful of spinach

Trim the carrots and cut them into 2- to 3-inch pieces. Beginning and ending with the carrot pieces, process the vegetables in the juicer.

Diverticula Tonic
Carrot-Cabbage-Apple Juice

One serving about 8 ounces

Any juice containing cabbage soothes the stomach—as long as it is mixed with milder juices such as carrot and apple.

5 carrots

1 (3-inch) wedge of green cabbage

½ apple

Trim the carrots and cut them into 2- to 3-inch pieces. Cut the cabbage and apple into narrow wedges. Process the vegetables and apple wedges in the juicer.

Eye Beautifier Juice
Carrot-Collard Greens/Carrot-Kale/Carrot-Mustard Greens/Carrot-Parsley Juice

One serving about 8 ounces

F or clear eyes that don't look red or irritated, try one of these juices.

6 carrots

1 large handful of collard greens or kale or mustard greens or parsley

Trim the carrots and cut them into 2- to 3-inch pieces. Process the vegetables in the juicer.

Note: Mustard greens have a potent oil that can taste very strong. Use them only in small amounts.

Fennel-Apple Juice

One serving about 8 ounces

Growing up in a Yugoslavian household, I ate a lot of fennel and so have always liked the flavor. This is also a fine tonic for an upset stomach.

4 ounces of fennel (1 small or ½ large bulb)

3 apples

Cut the fennel and apples into narrow wedges. Process them in the juicer.

Fennel-Beet-Apple Juice

One serving about 8 ounces

Wonderfully nutritious, this drink bears the distinctive flavor of fennel. The combination may relieve indigestion and help soothe an upset stomach.

6 ounces of fennel (1 medium bulb)

¼ beet with the greens

2 apples

Cut the fennel, beet, and apples into narrow wedges. Process the vegetables and apple wedges in the juicer.

Garden Salad Juice
Carrot-Cabbage-Lettuce Juice
(alkaline drink)

One serving about 8 ounces

If you tend a vegetable garden, use your own produce to make this refreshing juice. From the ground to your sink to your juicer to your body—that is what I call satisfying.

4 to 5 carrots

1 (3-inch) wedge of green cabbage

7 to 8 lettuce leaves

Trim the carrots and cut them into 2- to 3-inch pieces. Cut the cabbage into narrow wedges. Process the vegetables in the juicer.

Graying Hair Remedy
Cabbage-Spinach-Carrot Juice

One serving about 8 ounces

This won't keep the snow from the roof forever, but it may help ward off premature graying.

1 (3- to 4-inch) wedge of cabbage

Handful of spinach

4 carrots

Cut the cabbage into narrow wedges. Trim the carrots and cut them into 2- to 3-inch pieces. Process the vegetables in the juicer.

Green Power

Carrot-Celery-Spinach-Parsley Juice
(calcium drink)

One serving about 8 ounces

Reap the benefits of these vegetables by drinking them all together.

> 4 carrots
>
> 2 stalks of celery
>
> Handful of spinach
>
> Handful of parsley

Trim the carrots and cut them into 2- to 3-inch pieces. Cut the celery into 2- to 3-inch pieces. Process the vegetables in the juicer.

Hair Growth and Hair-Loss Prevention Tonic

Carrot-Alfalfa Sprout-Lettuce Juice

One serving about 8 ounces

Having trouble keeping a full head of hair? Try this—you'll like it. No one knows what really works and what doesn't. But a lot of people have thanked me for this juice recipe— and they all had plenty to run a comb through.

5 to 6 carrots
Handful of alfalfa sprouts
4 lettuce leaves

Trim the carrots and cut them into 2- to 3-inch pieces. Wrap the sprouts in the lettuce leaves to make neat packages for juicing. Process the vegetables in the juicer.

High-Potassium Drink
Carrot-Asparagus-Celery Juice

One serving about 8 ounces

Potassium, an essential mineral, maintains muscle tissue and may help relieve cramping.

4 carrots

1 to 2 stalks of asparagus

1 stalk of celery

Trim and cut the carrots, asparagus, and celery into 2- to 3-inch pieces. Process the vegetables in the juicer.

Idaho Trailblazer
Potato-Carrot-Apple-Parsley Juice

One serving about 8 ounces

The potato makes this combination—one of my favorites, as you know—even more healthful.

1 (1-inch) slice of potato

4 carrots

1 apple

Handful of parsley

Slice the potato into strips, if necessary. Trim the carrots and cut them into 2- to 3-inch pieces. Cut the apple into narrow wedges. Process the vegetables and apple wedges in the juicer.

Jay's Best
Carrot-Apple-Parsley Juice

One serving about 8 ounces

Very early on I began adding parsley to my all-time-favorite carrot-apple combination. I can't speak highly enough of the result—in our house we drink it almost every day.

5 carrots

1 apple

Handful of parsley

Trim the carrots and cut them into 2- to 3-inch pieces. Cut the apple into narrow wedges. Process half the carrot pieces in the juicer. Process the parsley and then the remaining carrot pieces in the juicer. Process the apple wedges. Mix well.

Jay's Secret
Carrot-Celery-Parsley-Garlic Juice

One serving about 8 ounces

Besides this being one of my longtime favorites, Linda and I and the boys drink this to fight infections and to help build our immune systems. You can't beat the power of garlic!

6 carrots

2 stalks of celery

Handful of parsley

2 cloves of garlic

Trim the carrots and cut them into 2- to 3-inch pieces. Cut the celery into 2- to 3-inch pieces. Beginning with the garlic, process the vegetables in the juicer.

Jay's Tomato Cooler
Tomato-Cucumber-Celery-Lime Juice

One serving about 8 ounces

Try this refresher on hot summer days when the garden's tomatoes are at their peak. The cucumber is a natural coolant and mixing it with the other ingredients is smashing.

1 large, ripe tomato

½ cucumber

1 stalk of celery

1 small slice of lime

Cut the tomato into narrow wedges. Cut the cucumber into quarters and cut the quarters into strips. Cut the celery into 2- to 3-inch pieces. Process tomato and the vegetables and lime slice in the juicer.

The Juiceman's Power of Juicing

131

Jicama-Carrot-Parsley Juice

One serving about 8 ounces

*H*ere's a jicama-based juice that soothes upset stomachs and indigestion while providing a good dose of calcium and phosphorus.

1 (1-inch) slice of jicama

6 to 7 carrots

Handful of parsley

Slice the jicama into strips, if necessary. Trim the carrots and cut them into 2- to 3-inch pieces. Process the vegetables in the juicer.

Jicama Jig
Jicama-Carrot-Apple-Celery Juice

One serving about 8 ounces

Try this if you feel a little queasy. You'll feel like dancing! This is great before plane trips, boat cruises, and roller-coaster rides!

1 (1-inch) slice of jicama

4 carrots

1 apple

1 stalk of celery

Slice the jicama into strips, if necessary. Trim the carrots and cut them into 2- to 3-inch pieces. Cut the apple into narrow wedges. Cut the celery into 2- to 3-inch pieces. Process the vegetables and apple wedges in the juicer.

Liver Mover
Apple-Beet Juice

One serving about 8 ounces

Because of the rich, red color, our boys have always been fond of this nutritious drink.

½ beet with the greens

3 to 4 apples

Cut the beet and apples into narrow wedges. Process them in the juicer.

Lung Tonic

Carrot-Parsley-Potato-Watercress Juice

One serving about 8 ounces

I drink this to help clean my lungs of toxins caused by air pollution. This is so delicious you will be sad when your glass is empty.

5 carrots

4 sprigs of parsley

1/4 potato

4 sprigs of watercress

Trim the carrots and cut them into 2- to 3-inch pieces. Cut the potato into narrow wedges. Process the vegetables in the juicer.

Nail Beauty Juice

Cucumber-Carrot-Kale-Green Bell Pepper Juice

One serving about 8 ounces

The calcium content in these vegetables helps keep nails strong and healthy.

1 small cucumber

4 carrots

3 kale leaves

¼ green bell pepper

Cut the cucumber into quarters and cut the quarters into strips. Trim the carrots and cut them into 2- to 3-inch pieces. Process the vegetables in the juicer.

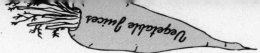
Vegetable Juices

Pacific Prize
Carrot-Cauliflower-Bok Choy Juice

One serving about 8 ounces

The high-mineral and magnesium content of this enhances endurance and stamina. Drink it if you work out regularly—and even if you don't! (Bok choy is a wonderful vegetable that you can usually find at Asian grocery stores.)

4 carrots

2 to 3 cauliflower florets with stems

½ leaf of bok choy

Trim the carrots and cut them into 2- to 3-inch pieces. Slice the cauliflower florets and stems into strips, if necessary. Process the vegetables in the juicer.

Pancreas Rejuvenator
Carrot-Apple-Lettuce-String Bean-Brussels Sprout Juice

One serving about 8 ounces

W hat is good for the pancreas is good for the entire body. I recommend this juice to everyone.

4 carrots

1 apple

4 to 5 lettuce leaves

3 ounces of string beans
(approximately ¾ cup)

3 ounces of Brussels sprouts
(approximately 3 to 4 sprouts)

Trim the carrots and cut them into 2- to 3-inch pieces. Process the carrot pieces in the juicer and set aside.

Cut the apple into narrow wedges. Process the apple wedges, lettuce leaves, string beans, and sprouts in the juicer. Combine the juices and mix well.

Pick-Me-Up Energy Cocktail
Carrot-Parsley Juice

One serving about 8 ounces

Our boys drink this to revive their energy. Linda and I drink it after they have gotten their energy back!

6 carrots

5 sprigs of parsley

Trim the carrots and cut them into 2- to 3-inch pieces. Process the carrot pieces and parsley in the juicer.

Pineapple-Celery Juice

One serving about 8 ounces

After a long trip this juice always seems to soothe my nerves. Just the thought of it calms me—and you should see how relaxed I get after a whole glass.

2 (1-inch-thick) pineapple rounds, preferably organic

2 stalks of celery

If the pineapple is not organic, remove and discard the skin. Cut the rounds into strips. Cut the celery stalks into 2- to 3-inch pieces. Process the pineapple strips and celery pieces in the juicer.

Popeye's Pop
Carrot-Beet-Spinach Juice
(alkaline drink)

One serving about 8 ounces

The sailor man munched on spinach for good reason. This will help you build strength and stamina too. (Please note: this recipe does not include Olive Oyl.)

4 carrots

1 beet with the greens

Large handful of spinach

Trim the carrots and cut them into 2- to 3-inch pieces. Cut the beet into narrow wedges. Process the vegetables in the juicer.

Red Pepper Ringer
Carrot–Red Bell Pepper–Parsley Juice

One serving about 8 ounces

The combination of carrots and red bell peppers heralds good news for all those interested in providing their bodies with lots of beta carotene.

4 carrots

2 to 3 strips of red bell pepper

½ handful of parsley

Trim and cut the carrots into 2- to 3-inch pieces. Process the vegetables in the juicer.

The Red Roar
Carrot-Apple-Beet Juice

One serving about 8 ounces

Linda and I consider this one of the best juices for flavor and healthfulness—well worth "roaring" about. The sweeter the apple, the tastier this drink will be.

5 carrots

1 apple

¼ beet with the greens

Trim the carrots and cut them into 2- to 3-inch pieces. Cut the apple and beet into narrow wedges. Process the carrot pieces and apple and beet wedges in the juicer.

Santa Fe Sunshine
Jicama-Pear-Apple Juice

One serving about 8 ounces

Deliciously fruity, this juice shares the tastiness—and benefits—of apples and pears with those of jicama.

1 (1-inch) slice of jicama

1 pear

1 apple

Slice the jicama into strips, if necessary. Cut the pear and apple into narrow wedges. Process the jicama and fruit in the juicer.

Satin Skin Juice
Carrot-Apple-Ginger Juice

One serving about 8 ounces

This combo is good for colds and nausea, and it also contributes to smooth, elastic skin. It's great for a boost in the morning. And the ginger makes it taste glorious. A real renaissance juice!

5 carrots

1 apple

½-inch knobs of gingerroot

Trim the carrots and cut them into 2- to 3-inch pieces. Cut the apple into narrow wedges. Slice the gingerroot, if necessary. Process the carrot pieces, apple wedges, and ginger in the juicer.

The Skin Cleanser

Carrot-Green Bell Pepper-Kale-Spinach-Turnip Greens Juice

One serving about 8 ounces

I believe this juice does more for your skin than a dozen facials. Try it in all its combinations.

6 carrots

1/2 green bell pepper

Plus

Handful of kale

1/2 handful of spinach

1/2 handful of turnip greens

or

Handful of spinach

1/2 handful of kale

1/2 handful of turnip greens

(continued)

or

Handful of turnip greens

½ handful of kale

½ handful of spinach

Trim the carrots and cut them into 2- to 3-inch pieces. Cut the green bell pepper into strips. Process the vegetables in the juicer.

Sweet Beet Juice
Carrot-Apple-Beet-Parsley Juice

One serving about 8 ounces

*A*dding parsley to this combination makes it even better. Don't forget the power of greens. All life on this planet comes from the greens!

4 carrots

1 apple

½ beet with the greens

Handful of parsley

Trim the carrots and cut them into 2- to 3-inch pieces. Cut the apple and beet into narrow wedges. Process the vegetables and apple wedges in the juicer.

Sweet Potato Magic
Carrot-Sweet Potato Juice

One serving about 8 ounces

This juice combines two of the best sources of beta carotene on the face of the earth—and it tastes terrific!

6 carrots

1 (1-inch) slice of sweet potato

Trim the carrots and cut them into 2- to 3-inch pieces. Process the vegetables in the juicer.

Waldorf Salad Juice
Apple-Celery Juice

One serving about 10 ounces

7he mixture of apple and celery is one of my longtime favorite combinations. This is a very healthy and relaxing evening drink.

4 apples
2 stalks of celery

Cut the apples into narrow wedges. Cut the celery into 2- to 3-inch pieces. Process the apples wedges and celery pieces in the juicer.

Zippy Spring Tonic
Pineapple-Radish-Dandelion Greens Juice

One serving about 8 ounces

This will get you going after a long winter! It is perfect before you tackle your spring cleaning.

2 (1-inch-thick) pineapple rounds, preferably organic

3 radishes

Handful of dandelion greens

If the pineapple is not organic, remove and discard the skin. Cut the rounds into strips. Process the pineapple strips, radishes, and dandelion greens in the juicer.

5

Fruits and Vegetables
—and Why They Are
So Good for You

There are so many fresh fruits and vegetables on the earth I cannot begin to cover them all. With modern technology and improved horticultural practices, new varieties are developed at an amazing rate. The flip side of this technology is the overuse of chemicals in the forms of pesticides and herbicides—toxins that can be harmful to man and beast. I encourage you to shop at markets and grocers that stock organic produce if at all possible. The flavor and overall goodness of the fruit or vegetable is better, although it may not look as picture-perfect as the produce grown for mass consumption by megafarmers. Those corporate giants use deadly chemicals to ensure that their crops are uniformly sized, ripen when it is most convenient, and do not spoil after even weeks or months in cold storage.

Organic produce does not keep as long—but since you buy it in season and often from a local farmer, it is fresher when you bring it home, and so much better for you and your family. (Many of the better supermarkets are now setting aside special sections for organic produce.) There are two kinds of organic produce: certified organic and transition organic. Certified organic vegetables and fruits are grown in soil that has not been exposed to pesticides for three years or longer. Transition organic produce is grown by farmers who are changing their growing methods and halting the use of sprays and other pesticides but have not yet met the three-year standard. Organic fruits and vegetables may not have the same bright color or perfect shape as nonorganic, but that is nature's way. In this case I prefer substance to form.

Beginning with fruits, I list some of my favorite fruits and vegetables to juice. With each one I outline its essential health benefits and provide you with shopping and storing tips. This is not an exhaustive list and some of your favorites may be missing, but each fruit and vegetable included here has a special place in my heart and contributes in its own way to vigorous health and general well-being. I hope you will try them all, and experiment with others. I suggest that before setting out for the market you read the advice I give on organizing fresh produce in the natural kitchen (pages 33 to 34). With few exceptions, which are noted in this chapter, washing and drying fruits and vegetables right after you get home is the best way to make sure you will follow the juice diet. Juicing is so much easier if you are organized, and the number one way to ensure this organization is to have the produce clean, dry, and ready the minute you feel the urge for fresh, frothy juice.

For over a hundred recipes using these fruits and vegetables, turn to page 44, where you will find delicious, healthful juices that will start you on the path to a more vigorous life.

Fruits

As I've stated elsewhere in the book, fruits energize and cleanse the body. For many beginning juicers, fruits are more fun and pleasant to juice than vegetables. The flavor of apple or orange juice is familiar; the idea of cantaloupe juice is appealing. But you will quickly discover that comparing the apple juice flowing from the juicer to the apple juice you pour from a jar is akin to comparing a live performance of the New York Philharmonic to a scratchy recording on an old seventy-eight.

A word of warning about fruit juices. They are high in natural sugars and should be consumed sparingly by anyone who has been advised to limit sugar intake. This may include people with diabetes, hypoglycemia, hyperglycemia, candidiasis, and gout. If you limit sugar intake, check with your doctor before incorporating fruit juices into your diet. The common recommendation is no more than sixteen ounces spread throughout a week. Other recommendations may include drinking fruit juices only with meals or diluting them with water. Be sure to follow your doctor's instructions and monitor your blood glucose closely.

Apples. Thought for centuries to have rejuvenation powers, apples were touted by civilizations in antiquity as diverse as those of the Norse and Turks. Only thirty varieties were recorded in ancient Rome, yet today there are more than fourteen hundred different types of apples. Some of my favorites are Delicious (easy to digest), Golden Delicious, red Winesap, McIntosh, pippin, Granny Smith, Jonathan, and Rome Beauties.

All these apples are great for juicing and at least two or three varieties are always available regardless of the time of year. Apples are a terrific source of pectin, which forms a gel to remove toxins from the intestines and at the same time stimulates peristaltic and bowel activity. The potassium and phosphorus in apples help flush the kidneys and control digestive upsets. The natural sugar in this fruit produces acids that stimulate saliva flow and digestion. This is why it is wise to chew an apple well in order to break down the starches, sugars, and carbohydrates and begin the digestive process. Eating apples is good for you, no doubt about it, but juicing them is better.

I try to eat only organic apples. Often as many as eleven chemicals are used by apple growers who then wax the fruit to preserve it further. If I have to eat a waxed apple, I always peel it. Some growers use a chemical spray called daminozide which penetrates the fruit and cannot be gotten rid of by any amount of washing. Another dangerous chemical is Alar, which may be carcinogenic but is being used in lesser amounts or eliminated altogether since the well-publicized public outcry a few years ago.

When you buy organic apples, check them for worms. They won't harm you but you probably don't want one going through the juicer. The government allows commercial canners to use a certain percentage of wormy apples in every batch of juice they make. This is only one reason I do not recommend bottled or canned apple juice. The canneries also use old, disfigured, rotten fruit. Why should they care? They filter the juice and then boil it so that the consumer never actually knows what goes into the juice. It is also difficult to know how much juice is in a can of apple juice. Regulations controlling what is printed on labels are becoming stricter but are still not enforced, according to the Center for Science in the Public Interest. That watchdog organization did a survey a few years ago on more than a dozen commercial juices and discovered that in many the amount of juice was only about 10 percent. The rest was water and sugar.

If you must buy apple juice, never buy it if you can see through it. This means it is pasteurized, or cooked, and then filtered so that all the helpful enzymes are removed. Buy instead cloudy-looking juice with sediment on the bottom, which indicates the juice is unfiltered and so probably contains more nutrients.

Many people wonder what the difference is between apple juice and apple cider. Legally, there is no hard-and-fast rule delegating which should be labeled what. Often it is a regional distinction. In apple-growing regions such as the Northwest and Northeast, growers make fresh apple cider during apple-picking season. This is often unfiltered and almost always unpasteurized apple juice pressed from apples the orchards find too misshapen to sell or that have been grown specifically for sweet cider. Because it contains no preservatives and is not pasteurized, the cider ferments in a matter of a week or so. Health food stores and other vendors sometimes sell what is called natural apple juice, a product exactly like the apple cider sold at the local orchard in the autumn. As I already mentioned, most bottled and canned apple juice on the market is pasteurized and filtered to make it shelf stable and crystal clear. **Buying and storing:** Look for firm, crisp apples without soft spots or bruises. Soft, mealy apples do not juice well. Rinse the apples in cool water if they are organic or soak them in a biodegradable produce wash if they are not. Dry the apples well and store them in the crisper drawer of the refrigerator. Do not worry too much if you cannot remove all the wax; peel the most offensive waxed apples and juice the others so that the skin (and any wax) end up in the pulp receptacle.

Apricots. A Persian poet called these luscious fruits the seeds of the sun, and one bite of the small golden orbs explains why. I love apricots for their flavor but also because of the potassium and magnesium, two minerals that supply us with energy, stamina, and endurance. They contain iron for blood building and silicon for beautiful hair and skin. But it is their high concentration of beta carotene that makes them stand out. In the fruit category, only cantaloupe matches apricots for beta carotene content, and as such apricots are a great souce of carotenoids, which may help the body prevent cancer. If you can find fully tree-ripened apricots, the beta carotene has built to its highest level.   **Buying and storing:**   Select apricots that are firm but not rock-hard. The skin should be orangy-gold with a faint pink blush indicating sweetness, never green. Store them at room temperature for a few days or in the refrigerator. Remove the stones before juicing.

Bananas. Man has been eating these long, slender fruits without seeds for some four thousand years when they were first cultivated in India. It makes sense that twelfth-century Chinese herbal doctors prescribed bananas for convalescence given their high potassium content which benefits the heart and the muscular system. Of the soft fruits, bananas are second only to strawberries when it comes to overall mineral content.

Because they are so soft, bananas are difficult if not impossible to juice. This is where the blender comes in handy, as you can blend a banana with other juices to make smoothies and nectars. For instance, combine half a banana with apple-strawberry juice (page 84) or with pineapple-orange juice (page 73). **Buying and storing:** Underripe bananas are hard to digest and should never be eaten. Most bananas are picked green and often are gassed to ripen. Buy them green, if possible, which often indicates they have not been gassed. It's simple to ripen bananas by leaving them at room temperature for a day or two, but for full nutritional impact, put them and an apple in a paper bag and stow it in a dark, room-temperature place (under the sink, for instance). The chemical reactions of the two fruits form a natural gas that ripens the bananas so that they contain as much potassium as those permitted to ripen on the tree. This takes only a day or so, although very green bananas may require as long as three days. For more than twelve bananas, use two apples.

Cherries. If we all ate a bowlful of cherries every day, we might be a lot healthier. Frankly, I would have no trouble doing so, if only this fantastic fruit were in season all year long. The shiny, dark red to almost black orbs of sweet flavor are packed with minerals and vitamins and, once the pits are removed, make wonderful juice. Darker cherries contain more iron, magnesium, and potassium than lighter ones, and all are good sources of silicon and provitimin A. There is some evidence that black cherry juice helps prevent the buildup of plaque and therefore is a deterrent to tooth decay.

Cherries are of the same family as peaches, apricots, and plums, which explains their center pit. Most are available only in the early summer, peaking in July. Remove the pit before juicing either by slicing the cherry in half and lifting it out or by using a cherry pitter, a handy, inexpensive gadget sold in most housewares stores. Both sweet and sour cherries are available, and the sweet Bings and Royal Anns are recommended for juicing. Sour cherries are generally used for canning. **Buying and storing:** Unlike peaches and plums, cherries do not ripen once picked from the tree. Buy plump, firm cherries with an obvious sheen and good-looking stems, avoiding any that are rock-hard or, conversely, mushy. Store them in the refrigerator for two or three days and juice them as soon as you can. Wash cherries with a gentle, organic cleanser just before using.

Citrus fruits. Grapefruits, lemons, limes, oranges, and tangerines are considered semitropical fruits. They share some universal characteristics, which I will cover before describing the individual fruits.

As every schoolchild knows, citrus fruits are bursting with vitamin C. When you juice citrus fruits, the vitamin C will dissipate quickly. Clearly, orange and grapefruit juices should be drunk within minutes of juicing for optimal benefits. What about the bottled and concentrated frozen citrus juices in the supermarket? Read the labels carefully; they often say "vitamin C enriched." You will get some vitamin C if you drink them, but it is not the original vitamin from the fruit itself but instead a synthetic vitamin from a test tube.

When you put citrus fruits in the juicer, you can, as with other fruits, put the seeds and membranes directly in the hopper. Do not put orange, grapefruit, or tangerine rinds in the juicer. These are the only fruits that always must be peeled before juicing as the skins are difficult to digest and can cause problems in the colo-rectal area. For this reason I advise you against including orange, tangerine, or grapefruit peel (also called "zest" in many recipes) in any dish. However, the skins of both lemons and limes are digestible.

As much as I advise avoiding the colored skins of

grapefruits and oranges, I highly recommend that you eat the white rind and membranes. Leave these on the fruit when you peel it for juicing or eating to benefit from the naturally occurring vitamin C and bioflavonoids—named "vitamin P" by the late Hungarian Nobelist Dr. Albert Szent-Györgyi who discovered vitamin C. Combined with the vitamin C, bioflavonoids strengthen capillaries and blood vessels, help the body fight colds, and increase antiviral, anti-allergy, and anti-inflammatory activity. Citrus fruits supply a good amount of provitamin A as well. **Buying and storing:** Always buy citrus fruits well ripened. Florida oranges often look slightly green even when fully ripe; California and Arizona oranges tend to be bright orange. Unlike some fruits, citrus fruits do not ripen once they're picked and therefore claims of "tree-ripened fruit" are meaningless. They should all be tree-ripened. A citrus fruit should feel heavy, otherwise it might be old and dried out; and thick skins indicate a lot of skin and pulp and not much juice. For the most juice, buy heavy, thin-skinned fruits and store them loose in the refrigerator. Remember that the highest concentration of vitamin C is in the juice.

Grapefruits. The most flavorful grapefruits are grown in Texas and Florida with names such as Star Ruby and Ruby Red (Texas) and Indian River and Orchid Island (Florida). Pink grapefruits are sweeter and less acidic than white but both are great sources of vitamin C, calcium, phosphorus, and potassium. The acids in the fruit stimulate digestive juices, and evidence is surfacing suggesting that the agent that causes the sour flavor of the fruit may help fight certain cancers. Grapefruit juice also combats colds and reduces the incidence of gum bleeding. Grapefruits are less acidic than lemons and, strange as it may sound, are tolerated better than oranges by many people. **Buying and storing:** Look for smooth, thin-skinned, round, heavy fruit with a discernible sweet fragrance. The fruit should feel springy, not soft, and be flat at both ends.

Lemons. Lemons are one of the most beneficial of all citrus fruits. Their juice is a rich source of bioflavonoids and plays a major role in ridding the body of toxins. The high citric acid content means that a little lemon juice goes a long way and it is best mixed with other juices or with distilled or mineral water. For those who want to consume lemon juice daily, I recommend about a half a lemon with eight ounces of water. Try Jay's World Famous Lemonade (page 68) for one of the best thirst quenchers—not to mention natural diuretics—around. **Buying and storing:** Rough and pebbly skin indicates low juice content, and any green on the skin means that the fruit is more acidic than usual. Many lemons are treated with wax and chemicals, so it is necessary to clean them with a biodegradable produce wash before storing them in the refrigerator.

Limes. Like their close cousin the lemon, limes are a flavorful, tart, subtropical fruit. Limes contain vitamin C, bioflavonoids, and potassium. They are best added to juices in small amounts or used as a garnish. Try the Fruit Cooler (page 62) and Honeydew-Lime Juice (page 66) for two delicious juices that take full advantage of the tangy taste of this wonderful fruit. **Buying and storing:** Smooth, heavy fruit indicate juiciness. Pebbly, rough skins mean the fruit will be drier and less flavorful. Wash limes with a biodegradable produce wash before juicing and store in a cool, not cold, environment.

Oranges. Oranges are almost everybody's favorite citrus fruit. Hardly a person in the Western world has not had a glass of orange juice or eaten an orange. But did you know that as recently as the last century oranges were considered rare? Some of the first greenhouses in Europe were built to protect fragile orange trees from frost, which explains the quaint, old-fashioned term "orangerie." Here in the United States we grow some of the sweetest oranges in the world, surpassed only by those from Israel. Florida oranges have more juice than California fruit. (California varieties such as Valencia and navel are renowned as eating oranges.)

By law, orange juice sold in cartons and bottles in the supermarket is pasteurized, a process that kills life-giving enzymes. As I've already said, because most of the vitamin C dissipates shortly after the juice is made, many manufacturers add synthetic vitamin C to bolster the content. Still others add sugar for sweetening.

None of this is necessary if you juice your own oranges. A glass of fresh orange juice is one of life's delights—but not in the form you probably imagine. When Mother squeezed fresh orange juice for Sunday morning breakfast she simply rotated the halved oranges on a reamer or pressed them in a squeezer. This is not juicing. It is rubbing tissues against membranes and creating what I call orange water. It may taste terrific but has few of the health benefits of orange juice made in the juicer.

Five to six oranges yield about a pint of juice. First you must remove the skin but leave the white pith and membrane. Cut the oranges into sections and put them through the juicer. What emerges is a thick, foamy drink with a heavenly creamy color. It contains almost all of the oranges' food value. The sweet, delicious juice is rich in vitamin C, B complex, bioflavonoids, potassium, zinc, and phosphorus, as well as natural sugar. Consumed pure, it is a perfect balance of nutrients that will help protect you from colds, flu, bruising, and heart disease and strokes. What is more, the nutrients strengthen your blood vessels and capillaries and give you a better chance of living a long and healthy life. **Buying and stor-**

ing: As with other citrus fruits, buy thin-skinned, heavy fruit and store it in the refrigerator.

Tangerines. Tangerines and tangelos are classed as mandarins and are rather like loose-skinned oranges. They have a higher sugar content, lower free-acid content, and are excellent sources of vitamin B₁. One small tangerine has more usable vitamin C than some large oranges. Many people who have trouble tolerating oranges do well with tangerines. The nutrients in tangerines help fight certain viral infections and evidence shows that eating two a day during inclement weather helps ward off colds.

Tangerines and their sister fruits are available from late November through early February. Different varieties abound, with the most popular being satsuma, the sweet and nearly seedless fruit from Japan; kinnow, which is thin-skinned and harder to peel than satsuma; and clementine, which is larger, deeper-colored, and with coarser skin than satsumas and kinnows. The fruit called mandarins are small, deep-orange-colored with pebbly, loose skin which separates easily from the flesh. These are tart, very juicy, and have lots of seeds. Tangelos are the largest of this variety, as they are a hybrid fruit of tangerines and other citrus fruits. The best are called mineola or red tangelo and are a product of crossing a tangerine and a grapefruit. **Buying and storing:** All members of this family of citrus fruits should be bought in season, stored at room temperature or in the refrigerator, and eaten within a week of buying. You can juice them, and they need to be peeled first, but they are best when you eat them.

Cranberries. Years ago when I lectured in Florida about juice therapy, I suggested that people sweeten just-made cranberry juice with just-made apple juice. Soon after that, a commercial juice company introduced "cranapple" juice. I guess it does not take long for a good idea to enter the public—and commercial!—consciousness.

Drinking fresh cranberry juice is one of the best things for you. The tiny red berries contain quininic acid, better known as quinine, which is a powerful acid capable of penetrating the villi of the ileum and entering the liver. Once in the liver, the quinic acid converts to hippuric acid, which helps remove the purines, uria, uric acid, and toxins from the bladder, kidneys, prostate, and testicles. This is good news for American men, who face increasing risk of prostate cancer. Cranberries also help cleanse and heal the urinary canal, a reassuring note for the many women who suffer from chronic urinary tract infections.

There is more about these remarkable berries. Scientists are currently testing their properties as virus fighters. Visitors to equatorial regions take quinine pills to protect themselves against malaria. I find that a glass of fresh cranberry juice can sometimes knock out flu symptoms overnight—aches and pains and all. Anyone susceptible to colds should drink lots of it in the wintertime.

The trouble with drinking cranberry juice is that the quinine makes it bitter and with the first sip your mouth puckers up. The companies that bottle cranberry juice add sugar or other sweeteners to make it drinkable. But this is unnecessary. Simply combine the juice with another, sweeter fruit juice such as apple, pear, or grape.

Cranberries are harvested in cranberry bogs in the Northeast, Northwest, and Great Lakes states. The native American fruit has changed little in appearance and nutritional value since the days of the first settlers and is grown and picked in much the same way as it has been for centuries. Cranberries ripen in late autumn, which puts them in the stores in November and December—just in time for the holidays. **Buying and storing:** Buy cranberries fresh whenever possible, making sure you get plump, firm, brightly colored berries. They generally are sold in twelve-ounce sacks and I recommend buying as many as you can carry. They freeze well so you can have delicious, healthful cranberry juice all winter. It is preferable not to wash cranberries until just before using them.

Grapes. The only thing I can imagine more wonderful to behold than a bowl of ripe, juicy grapes is a glass of fresh grape juice made with the stem and all. Sweet, nourishing grapes have been called the food of the gods and man has praised them since ancient times. Grape seeds were found in Egyptian tombs and Old Testament Bible stories talk of grape cultivation.

Today, most table grapes are imported from Central and South America, although we in the United States grow our share, as well as plentiful crops of wine and raisin grapes. There are between forty and fifty grape varieties, ranging in color from green and white to red and purple. Many are seedless, all are delicious.

Grapes are rich in potassium, a mineral that strengthens the alkaline reserves in the body while helping to stimulate kidney function and regulate the heartbeat. They are also a source of iron which builds hemoglobin in the blood. They stimulate digestive juices, promote action in the bowels, cleanse the liver, and eliminate uric acid from the body. What is more, they soothe the nervous system as few other fruits do. In France, many people eat nothing but grapes during their season as a natural way to cleanse and establish an alkaline-acid balance in the body. Some studies point to a lower incidence of cancer in the regions of France where the grape mono-diet is practiced yearly.

If you are diabetic, hyperglycemic, hypoglycemic, or have another blood sugar problem, you should avoid grapes and grape juice, as their high sugar content is not good for anyone with abnormal blood sugar levels. Conversely, this natural sweetness is what makes them so appealing to children and adults alike.

If the grape juice you make is too sweet—and believe it or not, it might be—add a little lemon juice to smooth it out. Mix it with other fruit juices or drink it straight. **Buying and storing:** If possible buy organic grapes. Grapes are among the most oversprayed of all fruits, sometimes being host to as many as forty-three different pesticides and chemicals. I buy only organic grapes for my sons—nothing is too good for them, even if the grapes cost as much as five dollars a pound. Grapes should be fresh, plump, firm to the touch, and well colored. If buying green grapes, look for a slightly yellow cast; red and purple grapes ought to be deeply colored throughout. The grapes should clearly "bloom," which is determined by a faint powdery appearance. When you pick up the bunch, few grapes should fall off or be leaking, shiny, or mushy. The stems should be green and alive-looking. Dried-up, brown stems indicate old grapes.

Wash grapes well and when they are dry, store them in the refrigerator where they will keep for a week or more. One of my favorite recipes is called Christmas Cocktail, a heavenly combination of apple, grape, and lemon (page 54). Other than in fruit juice mixtures, grapes and grape juice should be consumed by themselves and not when other food is eaten so you can benefit from their full nutritional goodness.

Kiwifruits. The kiwifruit was developed in New Zealand from a smaller, less tasty fruit, the Chinese gooseberry. So pleased were the New Zealand farmers with their creation, they named the fruit after their country's flightless national bird, the kiwi. Nowadays, kiwis are grown in California and because our growing season is at the opposite time of year from that "down under," the California crop dovetails nicely with the New Zealand imports so that kiwifruits are available all year long. This is excellent news since kiwis are rich in vitamin C and very juicy. The outside of the small, oval fruit is brown and fuzzy; inside the flesh is sherbet green with edible jet-black seeds. The flavor of kiwi has been compared to a combination of strawberries and pineapples. Cut the unpeeled fruit into pieces and juice them. Fantastic! I especially like to combine grape and kiwifruit juices in equal measure. **Buying and storing:** Buy firm kiwis that give slightly when pressed. They should not be rock-hard. Store them in the refrigerator, where they will keep for more than a week.

Mangoes. More of the world's population recognizes a mango than recognizes an apple. This fact, once grasped, should help you understand why there are so many varieties of the fruit. Mangoes are grown in Asia, South and Central America, the Caribbean, and Florida and California. They are among the most succulent and delicious fruits on the planet—although if you are unfortunate enough to get a poor specimen, you might disagree as a taste resembling turpentine fills your mouth. But keep looking and tasting. Most mangoes are sweet and wonderful and make flavorful additions to any number of juices. What is more, they are rich in beta carotene, potassium, vitamin C, and pantothenic acid, part of the B complex. Be sure to peel mangoes and remove the large inside pit before juicing. **Buying and storing:** Mangoes come in all sizes, although I prefer the larger varieties which often are juiciest. Haitian and Central American mangoes are in the markets as early as January, with the Florida crop taking over in the summer. The smooth skins are yellowish green, sometimes with a rosy hue. Ripe fruit yields slightly when pressed, as an avocado does, and the stem end should have abundant sweet fragrance. If there is no aroma, there is probably little flavor. Avoid fruit that is bruised, too hard or too soft, and smells of fermentation. Because mangoes are tropical fruits, they do not do too well in the refrigerator, although once ripe, they may be cut up and stored there for a day or two. Let mangoes sit at room temperature for a day or so to ripen fully and then juice or eat the luscious fruit.

Melons. All melons make delicious, creamy, energy-boosting juices. Their root systems reach deep into the nutrient-rich soil and pull water from far below the surface into these incredibly nutritious fruits. This renders all melons with a high density of nutrients in relation to their caloric count.

I urge you to eat melon and to drink melon juice by itself. On television and during seminars I will often say, "Eat melons alone or leave them alone," meaning that for their full food value, they should be digested without interference from other foods. Melons are excellent tonics and help with elimination of waste from the body. Because of their diuretic properties they are good for kidney problems.

When you juice melon you get much more than help with elimination. Juicing extracts valuable vitamins and minerals from the rind so that instead of getting about 5 percent of the melon's nutritional benefits, you get 95 percent. That's quite a difference! For instance, from the green rind of a water-melon, we get chlorophyll, provitamin A, protein, and potassium. From the juice of the white inner rind, which will give you a stomachache if you attempt to eat it, we get zinc, more potassium, iodine, and vitally important nucleic acids and enzymes that aid with digestion.

Cantaloupes. You may not realize it but cantaloupe heads the chart as the most nutritious fruit. I have long touted the amazing properties of these melons and my beliefs were confirmed by a list of fruits grouped by nutritional value compiled by the Center for Science in the Public Interest, a privately funded consumer health advocacy organization. After cantaloupe, watermelon comes in at a close second followed by oranges, strawberries, grapefruit, pineapples, tangerines, and peaches. Plums bring up the rear.

Cantaloupe is high in provitamin A and vitamin C as well as myoinositol, a lipid that relieves anxiety and insomnia and helps prevent hardening of the arteries. It contains the largest amount of digestive enzymes of any fruit, surpassing papayas and mangoes. Finally, these marvelous melons are recommended by the American Cancer Society as healthful agents in the battle against intestinal cancer and melanoma.

Cantaloupes are in season all summer long and into the fall. Eat as many as you can. An average-size melon contains only 100 to 110 calories, but the important density of nutrients per calorie is phenomenal. When you juice a cantaloupe, rind and all, you are getting nearly 100 percent of its food value—as opposed to 5 percent when you eat just the orange flesh. **Buying and storing:** Buy melons that have a smooth stem end with tiny cracks. The skin should be covered in netting and the melon should smell sweet. Keep them in the refrigerator if ripe, at room temperature if still a little firm.

Honeydews. White-colored and smooth-skinned, honeydew melons have beautiful light green, juicy flesh with a delicate, sweet flavor. Honeydew is a good source of vitamins C and provitamin A and potassium, zinc, and valuable digestive enzymes. **Buying and storing:** Look for melons with skins that are covered with a lightly patched netting and that have a discernible honey aroma. The melons that weigh about five pounds, have creamy yellow stem ends that give ever so slightly when pressed, are bound to be the sweetest, best-tasting. Avoid melons that are as hard as bowling balls. They will be just as hard inside and, because they were picked too early, will never ripen. Store honeydew at room temperature if you plan to eat it soon, or refrigerate it for a few days. Try honeydew juice with just a splash of lime (provided by juicing a slice of the citrus fruit).

Watermelons. When you understand the benefits of watermelon juice you can fully appreciate what I call the "juice advantage." Watermelon rind, both the green and white parts, is exceptionally nutritious, as I have said. Both are full of provitamin A, potassium, and zinc. Zinc fights impotency. It strengthens our bodies so that they are less susceptible to hernias and it cleanses the urogenital canal, as well as the kidneys and bladder while contributing to a healthy prostate. Watermelon is "tied" for the number one diuretic in the fruit world, close to cranberries. The juice advantage I mentioned becomes even more apparent when you realize that the watermelon rind releases a free-radical scavenger that reoxygenates cells, reverses the peroxide emission dying cells put forth, and effectively acts as an anti-aging agent.

I eat watermelon as often as I can. The sweet red flesh provides me with great mineral and tissue salts, needed fiber, and tastes wonderful on a hot day. But because 95 percent of the food value is in the rind, I juice this delicious fruit far more often than I eat it. Once you taste watermelon juice you will agree that it is the greatest thirst quencher around.

Buying and storing: Thump watermelons with your fingers to determine if they sound hollow and are therefore ripe. The skins, either green or green-and-white striped, should be dull rather than shiny and when you scratch them gently with your fingernails the green should come off easily. A wholesale grocer once told me to look for bee bites (stings) on the skin, those irregular markings indicating that bees have found the melon delightfully sweet. Some people also suggest checking the underbelly where the melon rested on the ground, as a pale color means the melon is "sweet and ready to eat." Or to juice. Store watermelons in a cool room or refrigerate if cut open.

Papayas. Who can say the name of this fruit without thinking of the tropics? In the imaginary belt that circles the globe below the Tropic of Cancer, papayas proliferate and people living there can pluck the fruit when perfectly ripe and enjoy them daily. We are not as lucky in most of the United States, but as shipping technology improves, we are seeing more and more papayas in the markets, some tasting nearly as delicious as the ripe fruit available in tropical climates. Most papayas sold in this country come from Hawaii and are round, green-yellow fruit weighing less than a pound. When cut open, the papaya is filled with juicy, soft flesh encircling a cluster of shiny, black, edible seeds.

Papayas make fine-tasting juice. The fruit is a good source of beta carotene, potassium, calcium, and vitamin C. Eaten rather than juiced, papayas are an excellent source of fiber. The fruit also contains the enzyme papain, which helps us digest protein. In fact, papain is used commercially to tenderize meat. **Buying and storing:** Try to buy fruit with some yellowing, which indicates that the papaya is approaching ripeness. Ripe fruit yields similarly to a mango or an avocado and should be stored in the refrigerator for only a few days. Unripe fruit will soften when left at room temperature for a day or two. Lightly speckled or spotted fruit tends to be more flavorful than more perfect-looking papayas, although this does not include rotten spots or obvious bruises. Be sure to peel the fruit before juicing.

Pears. I count pears among the most delicious and sensuous of fruits. The sweetness of a perfectly ripe pear is unsurpassed; the round shape and subtle shadings of green, yellow, brown, and rose have made pears a favorite with watercolorists and other artists for centuries. I can think of few better places to make use of this grand fruit than in the juicer. Because it is so thick and sweet, pear juice needs to be diluted with another juice, usually apple.

Pears are high in vitamin B₁ (thiamin), an important part of the B complex contributing to a healthy heart and a high energy level. They also are good sources of vitamin B₂ (riboflavin), B₃ (niacin), and folic acid, all important components of the B complex that contribute to overall cardiovascular health, even blood pressure, and physical performance. Pears contain a good dose of vitamin C and the minerals phosphorus, potassium, and calcium. Their sweetness is supplied in large part by levulose, a fruit sugar more easily tolerated by diabetics than others.

Even more than apples, pears are a first-rate source of pectin, an important aid in digestion and cleansing the body of toxins and other waste while stimulating peristaltic and bowel activity. As such, they are a good fruit to eat to curb constipation and improve digestion.

While pears have been cultivated for hundreds of years, only a handful of varieties are available in the everyday market. These include Bosc, Anjou, Bartlett, and Comice. Bosc pears are tan to brown and have a long, tapered neck. Their flesh is not as juicy as that of other pears. Anjous, readily available in the winter, have yellow-green skin and an oval shape and the blandest flavor of all pears. The most popular summer-into-fall pears are Bartletts with their bright yellow skin and sweet juiciness. I think Comice are the best-tasting pears—sweet, juicy, fuller, and rounder than the others with a mottled green skin that camouflages glorious flavor. Comice are available in the late fall through Christmas. **Buying and storing:** For eating, pears should feel slightly soft when pressed at the stem end. For juicing, the stem end must be firm without any give. Soft, ripe pears may clog the juicer. The juice of firm, hard (but not unripe) pears is as clear as apple juice, but even so the flesh is softer than other fruits and therefore I suggest juicing pears with firmer fruit, such as apple, beginning and ending with the firm fruit. This will ensure that the pear does not just turn to mush.

It is always a good idea to buy firm pears, as ripe ones may be bruised by other shoppers before you buy them. If you plan to eat the pears, store them at room temperature for a few days to soften and ripen. Pears for juicing are best kept in the refrigerator for up to a week.

Pineapples. With the first sip of fresh pineapple juice we are transported to a balmy, sun-kissed island where the trade winds rustle the palm fronds and gentle waves lap white crescent beaches. Drinking fresh pineapple juice does far more than remind us of the tropics, however. It is a fantastic source of the minerals potassium, chlorine, sodium, phosphorus, magnesium, sulfur, calcium, iron, and iodine. It is also rich in provitamin A, the B complex, and vitamin C. Too, it is a great source of bromelain, an enzyme that helps with digestion. If you eat animal products, even eggs, drink a glass of pineapple juice about thirty minutes after eating; the bromelain breaks down the amino acids so your digestion is eased. Bromelain also soothes the throat and often cures laryngitis.

I remember once when I was at Caesars Palace in Las Vegas and the performer scheduled to go onstage that evening had laryngitis. His bodyguard was an old buddy of mine from the days we played football at USC together. Knowing I was around, he asked my help. I suggested that the singer drink fresh pineapple juice all day long. By show time his voice was in fine form.

To prepare pineapple for juicing, after washing, scrubbing, and rinsing, lay the fruit on its side on a cutting board. First, twist off the spiny leaves on top and discard them. Next, cut the pineapple into 1-inch-thick rounds and then into strips. Absolutely leave the outside skin (if the fruit is organically grown) and inside core on the flesh. Juicing the entire fruit provides optimal nutrition. I juice pineapple every day of my life, mixing it in equal amounts with grapefruit juice. This is my morning drink and relieves the aches and pains caused by those old football injuries as nothing else can. **Buying and storing:** Buy pineapples with fresh, clean appearances, that are plump and large, feel heavy, and have leaves that pull out easily. The fruit should be a dark golden color and smell strongly of sweet pineapple. Because we think of pineapple as tropical, we may associate it with wintertime. It is true you can get nice, juicy fruit in the winter, but summer pineapples are the best. Even in Hawaii, the summer sun is strongest. Many pineapples in the markets are labeled "jet fresh" or "jet shipped" and have been flown from the pineapple fields just a day or two before you buy them. These cost more than other ones but are far fresher. Other pineapples are shipped by sea and then overland in refrigerated containers and may be several months old. Pineapples do not ripen once they are picked and old fruit can be woody and dry.

Pineapples should be kept at room temperature rather than in the refrigerator. If you cut one open and do not use all the flesh, trim it and store the juicy flesh in a glass container in the refrigerator. Eat or juice it as soon as you can.

Strawberries. All berries are good for you, but strawberries are the very best. The most apt way I can describe the flavor of freshly picked strawberries is that they taste of warm sunshine. Allowed to ripen naturally they are a fantastic source of vitamin C and natural sugars that cleanse the system. Strawberries are high in potassium and iron, which is good for strengthening the blood. The sodium content makes them a valuable tonic for nerves and for keeping glands healthy, which explains why they are considered "youth" food. If you break out in hives when you eat strawberries, you might be reacting to ones that are not fully ripe. Consult your doctor about whether you should try berries that you know are left on the plants until fully ripe.

What I value most in strawberries is the presence of ellagic acid, which reduces and often neutralizes the damaging effects of the carcinogen PAH found in cigarette smoke. If you find yourself in a room with a smoker—or if you are a smoker yourself—pop a few strawberries in your mouth during the time you must endure the smoke. Ellagic acid has been shown (in a study by Dr. Paul La Chance of Rutgers University) to dissolve the PAH. This is almost more important for nonsmokers than smokers, as breathing secondhand smoke is as harmful, or perhaps more harmful, as smoking cigarettes.

Drinking strawberry juice is a terrific way to get the full benefits of these marvelous berries. Because the juice is quite thick, you might want to mix it with other juices to thin it. For instance, try it with grape (page 86) or pineapple juice (page 67). **Buying and storing:** Buy the freshest strawberries you can. If you live near a farm that grows them you can often pick your own during their early-summer season so that you are assured of sweet, juicy, sun-ripened berries. The longer they stay on the plant, the more vitamin C they contain—and the better they taste. Irrigated berries from the huge commercial farms in California and other agricultural states are less tasty than those grown on small farms but nevertheless are a good choice for regular juicing. You cannot beat the flavor of strawberries.

Select red, firm, fragrant berries with a slight shine and with the little green cap still attached. Wash them in cold water and dry them stem side down on absorbent paper or cloth towels. When they are dry, store the strawberries loosely in an open paper bag in the refrigerator for a few days.

Vegetables

Before beginning my discussion of vegetables, I want to reiterate three points:

First, I tend to be a vegetarian when I juice, a fruitarian when I eat. This does not mean I do not enjoy fresh, frothy fruit juices made from the fruits I have described. Absolutely not. I drink an average of two glasses of fruit juice a day, but I drink four glasses of vegetable juice a day. I believe vegetable juice is essential for robust health. Nutrients supplied by vegetables are the body builders, and ingesting them in concentrated form—as juice—ensures strong, healthy bodies free of a myriad of aches, pains, and more serious complaints experienced by those not eating healthfully.

However, there are some people who should take care when incorporating juice into their diet. Anyone prone to kidney stones should eliminate juices made from high-oxalate foods such as spinach, beets, and collard greens.

Second, I urge you to "chew" vegetable juice. This may sound contradictory, but as I explained earlier, you receive the most benefits from fresh vegetable juice if you swirl it around in your mouth for thirty to sixty seconds before swallowing. As the juice warms to body temperature in the mouth, it becomes sweeter-tasting. More important, the warm juice stimulates and mixes with a digestive enzyme in the saliva called ptyalin. This process accelerates digestion and ultimate absorption.

Third, because of their concentrated nutrients, never drink green juices alone. Green juices are derived from leafy, obviously green vegetables such as lettuce, cabbage, broccoli, greens (mustard, collard, etc.), and spinach. The juice is too potent for the body to handle and, while not causing lasting damage, may result in light-headedness and abnormal bowel movements for a day or two. When you juice green vegetables, make sure only about a quarter of the glass contains green juice. Fill it the rest of the way with carrot-celery-apple juice or a similar combination.

Asparagus. Most plentiful in the early spring, asparagus is increasingly available much of the year. Buy it whenever you can, knowing that it is most beneficial when in season and therefore freshest. Asparagus is pricey because cultivation is labor-intensive—if you have ever tried to grow it in the garden you know that it takes at least three years to establish a bed and thereafter the raised beds require watchful care. Even so, wild asparagus grows along grassy tracks and is a favorite of spring foragers here and in Europe.

The most valuable nutrient in asparagus is the alkaloid asparagine, the properties of which are largely destroyed by cooking. Asparagine stimulates the kidneys, is a powerful diuretic and blood purifier, and helps the bowels. It also soothes the nervous system. It is asparagine that causes many asparagus eaters' urine to turn dark and develop a strong odor. These symptoms are harmless and pass in a matter of hours. Asparagus is also a valuable source of beta carotene, vitamins B₁ and C, bioflavonoids, and potassium. Bioflavonoids work in tandem with vitamin C to strengthen capillaries and reduce the incidence of bleeding gums and related disorders. **Buying and storing:** Both thick- and thin-stalked asparagus is good for you. Either should be bright green and brittle with firm, tight tips. Asparagus keeps for only a few days in the refrigerator. Because it is a green juice, mix it with carrots and celery (page 127).

Beets. It is no coincidence that ruby-red beets are beneficial to the blood. Old-time raw foodists and herbalists have long known that the color or shape of a fruit or vegetable often conveys its healthful properties. Beets contain iron, calcium, sulfur, potassium, and chlorine. They also are a source of beta carotene and vitamin C. Their rich mineral makeup contributes directly to the well-being of the liver and gall bladder while building up blood corpuscles and cells and stimulating the activity of the lymph glands. Beets emulsify bile and flush the kidneys and bladder. Beet greens are rich in carotenoids which help prevent certain types of cancer. They also contain manganese, which combines with iron to feed the liver and red corpuscles. This vital mineral contributes to normal brain functions, reproductive functions, bone structure, and normal glucose metabolism.

Beet juice is potent stuff. Never drink it solo. Always dilute it with a milder juice such as apple (page 134), carrot (page 112), or cucumber (page 111). The juice of half a small beet is all that should be mixed with the juice of four apples. Pure beet juice—from the bulb or the greens—may temporarily paralyze your vocal chords, cause you to break out in hives, increase your heart rate, and give you alternating chills and fever. **Buying and storing:** Look for smooth, firm beets. Soft or shriveled beets may be woody and tough. I try to buy small beets, as they tend to be young and tender. Store them in the refrigerator or a cool room such as an unheated pantry or cellar.

Bell peppers. Mild-tasting bell peppers may be green, red, yellow, or nearly black. Indigenous to South and Central America, they were introduced by the Spaniards to Europe along with two other members of the nightshade family—tomatoes and potatoes—where their slightly sharp yet sweet flavor made peppers a favorite of Mediterranean cuisines. The most common bell peppers are green, readily available at supermarkets all year long. Red bell peppers are green peppers allowed to ripen on the vine—peppers do not continue to ripen once picked—and are much sweeter than green peppers. Yellow and black peppers are special varieties with sweet flavor and high price tags.

All peppers are good sources of beta carotene and vitamin C. Red peppers contain more vitamin C than less mature green peppers. Peppers also contain a good bit of silicon and so are beneficial in reducing swelling caused by tendinitis and very good for the skin, hair, and nails. Read the section on cucumbers for more information on the wonders of this mineral.

Bell peppers add a very distinct and dominant flavor to juices and I recommend using only a quarter of a medium-sized pepper for juicing with another vegetable such as carrots (page 142) or greens (page 146). The pepper is a terrific flavor booster and since it is a green juice, it must be mixed with other juices. **Buying and storing:** Buy firm, smooth-skinned peppers. If they are very shiny, they probably are waxed and should be avoided. Organic peppers may not have the perfect bell shape that gives the vegetable its name but are much better for you than nonorganic. Store peppers in the refrigerator.

Broccoli. This green vegetable has an abundance of beta carotene and is thus one of the best foods you can eat or drink. Beta carotene is a powerful cancer fighter. As one of the most common and best-tasting cruciferous vegetables, broccoli is a vegetable the American Cancer Society suggests we eat several times a week, stating that cruciferous vegetables "might reduce the incidence of colon, stomach and esophageal cancers."

Beta carotene is not the only good thing about broccoli.

The inexpensive and easily available vegetable is full of vitamins B, and C and has high amounts of calcium, sulfur, potassium, and traces of selenium (see the discussion of cabbage to learn the value of this important trace element). Plus, the National Cancer Institute recently identified a substance in broccoli called indol-3 carbonal that seems to emulsify estrogen in women and may reduce the risk of breast cancer. Mix broccoli juice with carrot (page 105) and apple juice (page 103).

The American Cancer Society urges you to eat broccoli. I also suggest you juice it and related vegetables as often as you can. If you eat it, eat it raw for fuller benefit of its valuable nutrients and fiber, even though it will not provide you with the same concentration of beta carotene, vitamins, and minerals that juicing will. You can consume far more in a single serving when you juice and will reap the benefits sooner. **Buying and storing:** Select heads with tightly clustered tops and no yellow florets. The stalks, which should be juiced right along with the clustered tops, should be firm with nice green leaves. Old broccoli has limp, woody stalks.

Brussels sprouts. These tiny heads of tightly wrapped leaves are the aristocrats of the cabbage family. But regardless of their elegance, Brussels sprouts are often maligned rather than being touted as one of the most nutritious foods you can eat.

Brussels sprouts are cruciferous vegetables similar in nutritional composition to broccoli (see the broccoli section). They contain a first-rate supply of vitamin C and calcium, sulfur and potassium. Their provitamin A content is slightly lower than that of broccoli, but their protein content is higher.

The combination of Brussels sprouts and string bean juice is a magnificent one. This drink can be beneficial for some diabetics and hypoglycemics. I am not advising that, if you are diabetic or hypoglycemic, you ignore your doctor's advice and your medication. But I am suggesting that you check with your doctor and then try adding Brussels sprout–string bean juice to your diet. These are both green juices and must be combined with other vegetable juices to make them palatable. I mix them with carrot and apple, sometimes adding a little parsley and lettuce (page 138). **Buying and storing:** Buy fresh Brussels sprouts, which are best in the late fall, when they are in season. The leaves should be dull green with no fading, yellowing, or wilting. The sprouts should not smell strong. Sometimes you can buy Brussels sprouts still attached to the stalk; do this if possible as this indicates freshness. Store Brussels sprouts in plastic bags in the refrigerator. Do not wash them until just before juicing.

Cabbage. Another cruciferous vegetable, cabbage is often overlooked by the modern homemaker or thought of only as the base for fattening, oily coleslaw or the slippery accompaniment to dried-out corned beef. When I was growing up in San Pedro, California, near the Los Angeles harbor, we ate cooked cabbage several times a week, as we were poor along with everyone else during the 1930s Depression. My Yugoslavian parents grew masses of cabbage in our tiny garden patch, along with other vegetables familiar to them. My mother boiled cabbage with oil, herbs, and garlic for an inexpensive (actually dirt cheap!) dish called *cupussa,* and while I now know that we were getting very little nourishment from the overcooked vegetable, it did fill our stomachs. But how can I forget the horrendous, sulfurous smell of the cooking cabbage? Boiled or steamed cabbage loses a portion of the vegetable's vitamins and minerals and what is left is inorganic sulfur. The dead sulfur settles in the pockets of the stomach and often causes extreme gastric distress.

Later I discovered the power of juicing and found that the staple of my childhood was a valuable vegetable for my diet. Cabbage is a good source of beta carotene, vitamin C, sulfur, and if grown in mineral-rich soil, selenium, a trace element that plays a big role as a cancer-fighting agent as well as protecting against heart disease and inflammatory conditions such as arthritis. Selenium, considered an anti-aging mineral, promotes healthy-looking skin and increases male potency. Cabbage also is inundated with the amino acid glutamine.

I had an interesting experience with this amino acid in the late 1940s when Dr. Garnet Cheney, who at that time headed the Cancer Division of Stanford Medical School in Palo Alto, California, invited me to instruct him and other doctors on the proper way to juice. Dr. Cheney was in the process of researching the value of glutamine in healing stomach ulcers. He theorized that stomach ulcers might be precursors to colo-rectal cancer. Working with sixty-five volunteers, all of whom suffered from stomach ulcers, we began intensive cabbage juice therapy. Each subject drank a quart of cabbage juice a day. Because the concentrated juice resulted in so much gastric upset, we changed the formula to cabbage-celery-carrot juice. Within three weeks, all but two of the patients were healed and the two holdouts had only minimal symptoms. Today research is under way investigating this amino acid's role in relieving or curing extreme colitis and curbing alcohol cravings. **Buying and storing:** Buy only cabbage heads that look healthy on the outside. Worm-eaten, decaying outer leaves indicate that the entire head may be infested with worms at worst, or at least is not fresh. Also, because the outer leaves contain many nutrients, it is counterproductive to have to discard them. I keep cabbage in the refrigerator for a week or longer. It also will keep in a cool, unheated room during the winter for several days. To make it palatable, I always mix cabbage juice with other juices, usually carrot or apple.

Carrots. What would I do without carrot juice? Along with apple juice, it is the most versatile of juices, combining well with and sweetening a host of others. Sweet, delicious carrot juice is brightly colored and easy to digest. Children like it as much as fruit juice and seem nearly always ready to drink a glassful. Linda and I generally stock fifty pounds of organic carrots every two weeks, storing this huge cache in a refrigerator in our garage. Believe me, the carrots disappear in that two-week period as both of us and our two sons down carrot juice with ferocious frequency.

Once you begin juicing you will find carrot juice becoming an integral part of your diet. Carrots are a terrific source of provitamin A (beta carotene)—an eight-ounce glass has about 20,000 milligrams of this nutrient. If you ingest vitamin A supplements (fish oil), your body can store too much and toxicity can occur. When you consume provitamin A from vegetables, overdosing is impossible. If your skin becomes slightly orange due to excessive carrot juice intake, do not be alarmed. This is harmless. A pound of carrots also contains about 30 milligrams of vitamin C, as well as most of the B complex. Besides calcium and iron, carrots contain the minerals potassium, sodium, and phosphorus.

The complex carbohydrates in carrots give the body energy. Carrot juice is also easy to digest. Its therapeutic effect on the liver cannot be overlooked as it assists the organ to release bile and excess cholesterol. Alkaline minerals in carrots soothe and tone the intestinal walls while protecting the entire nervous system. To me all of this adds up to make carrot juice the most balanced of all vegetable juices.

I drink lots of carrot juice, alone and mixed with other juices. It helps protect the skin against sunburn, a bonus for those of us who enjoy being outside in good weather. So beneficial has carrot juice been shown to be, I have heard that on nearly every corner of every commercial street in Israel you can buy carrot juice. People drink it for its delicious taste and because of its preventitive properties.

Once when I was making a television appearance for an NBC station, I met a man named David Lebowitz who asked me for a glass of carrot juice. He walked with a cane and stooped but otherwise seemed in good health. He told me that six years earlier he had been crippled by the onset of multiple sclerosis. Blind and paralyzed, he lay in bed trying to accept his fate. He lost his job as head of production at the television station, but he most missed playing with his young son. After two years, some friends finally took him to a spa in Baden-Baden, Germany, where he went on a carrot juice diet. His vision returned and he walked again. Nowadays, he works at the TV station feeding the teleprompter, drives, reads, walks, and generally enjoys his family and his life. I view Mr. Lebowitz's story as a testimony to the power of carrot juice.   **Buying and storing:** Buy firm, smooth carrots without cracks and bruises or small white roots. A thick mass of new sprouts or leaves at the stem end may indicate woody cores, as will diameters of more than one and a half inches. The brighter the color, the sweeter the carrot. Keep carrots in the refrigerator for up to two weeks. Nonorganically grown carrots should be cleaned well and trimmed at the top and the stem end by about a half inch. Pesticides concentrate in the stem end. Even if the carrots are dirty, do not peel them. A great portion of the food value lies just below the peel and scraping off the skin removes it. Instead, scrub the carrots under running water with a gentle scouring brush. Organically grown carrots need only to be rinsed before juicing. You don't have to trim them at all.

Cauliflower. Mark Twain called cauliflower "cabbage with a college education" and certainly the snowy white vegetable has many of the same nutritional benefits as cabbage. This crucifer has been grown in home vegetable gardens for centuries but was not harvested commercially until the 1920s when twentieth-century agriculture determined ways to cultivate the sensitive plant in the cool temperatures it prefers.

Cauliflower is a source of phosphorus and potassium. It contains indol-3 carbonal, which researchers are beginning to believe may help protect women against breast cancer.

Cooked cauliflower can cause unpleasant indigestion, and even raw can be difficult to digest. When I juice it, I usually combine it with carrots and parsley or with apple (pages 113 and 110). **Buying and storing:** Look for compact, firm heads of cauliflower with uniform pale-ivory-to-white color. The head should be surrounded by light green leaves. Avoid vegetables with brown spots or signs of mildew. Store cauliflower in the refrigerator or, if you will juice it in a day or two, a cool pantry or cellar.

Celery. This familiar, common, green stalk vegetable packs a powerhouse of life-giving nutrition. Celery juice is the best juice for anyone who works out, as it is a rich source of organic sodium. The human body, approximately 70 percent water, requires about two quarts of water a day, easily done with the juice added to your diet. When we sweat we lose a lot of valuable body fluids. How best to replace them in a matter of minutes? Drink celery juice—leaves and all!

I advise that you toss the salt shaker into the trash. You won't need it if you juice. By eating a balanced diet of juices, vegetables, fruits, grains, and legumes the body maintains a perfect balance of sodium-potassium in a 1:5 ratio. This ratio is echoed in one of the best juices you can drink: one rib of celery combined with two apples (page 150).

The sodium-potassium balance helps alleviate muscle cramping and fatigue on the playing field or in the office. At the same time, celery-apple juice relieves anxiety and stress and can be especially soothing for insomniacs. It is a fantastic tonic for headaches. Forget the aspirin; drink a glass of celery-apple juice—history tells us that even the ancient Greeks relied on celery for headaches. If, however, headache persists, consult a doctor. Celery-apple juice also cleanses the body of excessive carbon dioxide, which is especially important if you live in a polluted part of the country.

Celery juice cools the body and is a terrific drink during the hot weather—you won't need the air-conditioning on as much or as high. If you are dieting, celery juice curbs the desire for sweets.

For all these reasons, I list celery juice among the most important "youth" drinks. Consume it regularly and you will very likely lead a physically active life well into what some folks refer to as "old age." **Buying and storing:** Select firm, crisp stalks of celery with healthy-looking leaves. Limp, pliable ribs and glossy surfaces indicate that the celery was picked too many weeks ago. Store celery in the refrigerator.

Cucumbers. The expression "cool as a cucumber" has basis in fact. Cucumbers maintain an internal temperature about twenty degrees lower than the external temperature on a warm day. Because of this, people in hot regions such as India and the Middle East have been consuming cucumbers for centuries as natural coolants.

I consider cucumbers the watermelon of the vegetable family. As do watermelons, cucumbers contain a great amount of water and therefore help regulate body temperature and body processes by carrying nutrient-rich water to the cells and carrying waste from the cells.

High in potassium, sulfur, and manganese, cucumbers

also are an excellent source of chlorine and silicon. Silicon is beneficial to anyone suffering from tendinitis. It also rejuvenates muscles and gives elasticity to dermal cells and so is great for the complexion. Taken alone or, even better, combined with carrot, lettuce, or spinach juice, cucumber juice is delicious and may promote hair and fingernail growth and help prevent hair loss. Here is another "youth" juice and by drinking it regularly you will retain much of the vitality of youth.

I do not recommend drinking cucumber juice by itself only because it is a weird-tasting drink. I usually blend it with carrots and sometimes add a little beet juice too (page 100) as I was taught to do by my mentor, Dr. Norman W. Walker. **Buying and storing:** Buy firm cucumbers with dark green skins. Good cucumbers have small lumps on their surface but should never be wrinkled, scarred, or have soft spots. If the cucumbers are waxed, peel them before juicing. Otherwise, wash them carefully with a biodegradable produce wash. Store dry, cleaned cucumbers in the refrigerator.

Dandelion greens. You may consider the dandelions overtaking your lawn a nuisance. At best, you view the small, bright yellow flowers as a pretty weed that children pick, weave into charming wreaths and necklaces, and then when the flowers dry out, wish upon with a gentle, breathy blow. But these easy-to-gather plants are valuable additions to the juice diet.

The green leaves and the roots are great for juicing. I always juice them with another vegetable, usually a sweet carrot or two, because of their greenness and their bitterness, which increases as the summer progresses and the plants become more firmly entrenched and mature. If you do not fancy pulling up your lawn, buy dandelion greens at the market or greengrocer.

Because they taste mildest in the spring, dandelion-based juice has come to be considered an excellent spring tonic capable of cleansing the system and strengthening the blood and bones. An increase in consumption at this time of year is a good idea as most of us increase our physical activity as the days become balmier. Dandelion greens contain nearly as much iron as spinach and four times the provitamin A of lettuce. They are good sources of potassium, calcium, and sodium as well as vitamin C. Most important, they are a superior source of organic magnesium.

An article in the May 1990 issue of *Runner's World*, a magazine dedicated to fitness and running specifically, stated that depletion of magnesium reduced the body's natural ability for stamina and energy by as much as 30 percent. Those of us who have been studying and following a nutritious and balanced vegetarian diet for a number of years know this to be true. Magnesium alkalizes the bloodstream and at the same time contributes to bone density and health. It is vital for strong teeth and preventing tooth decay and pyorrhea. **Buying and storing:** Buy fresh-looking greens in the market and at the farm stand. Dandelion greens are sometimes easy to find at health food stores in season (late spring and early summer). Rinse them well, and if necessary, soak the greens in a biodegradable produce wash. Store them when perfectly dry in large Ziploc plastic bags and use them within a few days.

Fennel. Italians have been using fennel for generations, but a lot of people may be baffled by this odd-looking vegetable. You may have seen it in the market, resembling a bunch of celery that was run over by a truck, and topped with feathery, lacy leaves. Fennel has a distinctive licorice flavor, which surprises a lot of people who expect that taste only in candy.

Fennel belongs to the same family as celery and shares many of celery's health-giving properties. High in provitamin

A and vitamins B and C, fennel also is a good source of calcium, sulfur, and iron. When mixed with carrot juice, it is helpful for combating night blindness and other eye disorders. When beet juice is added to the carrot-fennel juice it becomes a viable blood strengthener and beneficial to menstruating women. I combined it with apple juice (pages 121 and 122) and discovered the drink was magnificent for indigestion and upset stomach—despite its unappealing brown color. Fennel juice has also been known to relieve the symptoms of migraines. **Buying and storing:** Always buy fennel with the leaves attached and healthy-looking. The bulb should be solid, crisp, and white with no visible yellowing. Like celery, fennel should be refrigerated and used within a week or so.

Garlic. Undoubtedly you have read a lot about garlic lately in newspapers and magazines. It seems everyone is discovering what vegetarians and holistic healers have known for centuries. Garlic is a powerful healer.

The pungent bulb is credited with all sorts of wonderful properties. There is evidence suggesting that garlic reduces blood pressure, lowers the incidence of blood clotting, reduces "bad" LDL cholesterol, prevents some stomach cancer, and boosts the immune system. It also may reduce the chance of having a second heart attack if it is ingested in fairly large amounts after recovering from the first. A component in garlic called allicin not only makes it smell, it most likely inhibits bacterial growth and destroys fungi and yeast in the body. This explains why it may be more beneficial to ingest natural garlic than to swallow an odorless garlic pills. Garlic also stimulates the flow of digestive enzymes and rids the body of toxins through the skin.

The amount of garlic we should consume is up for debate. I feel one or two cloves a day is a good idea. One clove of mild elephant garlic is the equivalent of about eighteen smaller ones. When I juice garlic, I run one or two cloves through the juicer and follow them with carrots, a little parsley, celery, beets, or apples. By the time the other vegetables (or apples) have gone through the juicer, the odor is removed from the machine. (For a recipe for garlic juice, see page 130.) **Buying and storing:** Buy garlic often so that you are assured of its freshness. Never buy it if it is soft or has black mildew on the papery skin. The heads should be composed of firm, plump cloves. Store garlic at room temperature in a well-ventilated container or basket. Never refrigerate it.

Gingerroot. Asians have been flavoring food with ginger since ancient times. Its medicinal properties have been touted for nearly as long. The knobby bulb causes superficial blood vessels to dilate so that at first you perspire and then feel cool. This makes ginger a good food to ingest if you have a fever.

Ginger is delicious mixed with apple juice and may aid in healing vocal chords if you have laryngitis. It also acts as an expectorant, helping rid the sinus cavities of mucus and the lungs of phlegm. Drink ginger-carrot juice often and especially if you feel a cold coming on. **Buying and storing:** Buy fresh gingerroot in the produce section of supermarkets and greengrocers. It should be dry and knobby with no soft spots or discernible odor. Store the root in a cool, dry place, much as you would garlic. Do not refrigerate it. If the skin seems especially tough, peel the ginger before juicing.

Greens. Collard, mustard, and turnip greens have nourished man for centuries, as wandering tribes from every continent relied on them as a staple of their diet. Greens are easy to grow and show up in gardens and untilled fields alike. But too often today they are discarded in favor of more tender lettuces and more commonly recognizable vegetables.

Greens are hard to digest if eaten raw in a salad. Many people cook them to soften the cellulose walls and while this may make the greens easier to chew, it kills many of the beneficial nutrients in them. All this is avoided with juicing. Most of the food value of the greens is absorbed into the body in a matter of minutes.

Some greens deliver more than 100 percent of the Recommended Daily Allowance (USRDA) of both vitamins A and C. Many also contain a significant amount of iron and calcium. Some of the most nutritious greens are kale, mustard greens, parsley, spinach, Swiss chard, and turnip greens. **Buying and storing:** Buy only greens with sturdy leaves. Avoid bunches with thick- or coarse-veined, flabby, yellowed leaves. Mustard greens may have a bronze tint. After soaking greens in a biodegradable produce wash, or rinsing them under cold water if they are organically grown, spin-dry the leaves. When they are completely dry, store them in large Ziploc plastic bags in the refrigerator. Juice greens as soon as possible, as they keep for only a few days. Remember, greens make green juice which must be combined with other juices such as carrot and celery.

Jicama. To many Americans, jicamas are as common as potatoes, but to many more they are unfamiliar. Pronounced "HEE-ka-ma," this tough-skinned tuber is native to Mexico and the rest of Central America and figures prominantly in the cuisines of that area. Jicamas are crisp and juicy with a flavor and texture similar to those of water chestnuts.

Jicamas are an excellent source of calcium and phosphorus. I combine jicama with carrot juice and parsley (page 132) and with carrot-apple-celery juice (page 133). Both juices soothe upset stomachs. Jicamas can be juiced with pears (page 144) (one exception to the no-fruit-but-apples-with-vegetables rule). This combination may also help soothe hemorrhoids. **Buying and storing:** Jicamas should be firm, free of soft spots and bruising. The tough outer skin should be peeled before eating—try sliced jicamas in salads—but can stay on when juicing. Store jicamas as you would po-tatoes, in a cool area.

Kale. The hardy curled leaves of kale announce it as a mem-ber of the mustard family, a close relative to cabbage, Brus-sels sprouts, cauliflower, and turnips. I think of it as headless cabbage with many of the same strengthening properties of cabbage and its other relatives. (Read the section on cab-bage to understand the full benefits of kale.) Like juice made from greens and lettuce, kale makes "green" juice and must be combined with other vegetable juices such as carrot and cucumber (see pages 101, 146, and 136).

Vitamin- and mineral-rich kale may protect against some cancers. It also helps relieve constipation, arthritis pain, and bladder problems. And kale is an excellent source of cal-cium. **Buying and storing:** Look for crisp, deep green kale without thick, coarsely veined leaves. Soak the leaves in a biodegradable produce wash or simply rinse the leaves if the kale is organically grown. After you spin-dry the leaves, store them in Ziploc bags in the refrigerator.

Lettuce. When I speak of lettuce I refer to leafy heads of romaine, Boston, Bibb, red- and green-leaf, and garden-variety leaf lettuce. I do not mean iceberg, also called head lettuce, the heavy, pale green heads that are overcultivated and nearly without food value.

Lettuce juice is rich in provitamin A and vitamin C as well as life-giving chlorophyll and the mineral silicon. It also has sulfur and chlorine, two cleansers that may lessen the chance of contracting lung cancer by smokers if consumed daily. The silicon helps hair health and growth and adds a glow to the skin. B complex vitamins, particularly folic acid and PABA, contribute as well to healthy skin.

Eaten raw, the roughage in lettuce helps with digestion. Lettuce is beneficial to teeth and gums as it sweeps over and cleans them during chewing. The food value is in the darkest leaves of any head of lettuce. A well-developed stem may indicate bitterness, but combining green lettuce juice with carrot and parsley (page 99) tempers the bitterness. In any event, never drink pure lettuce juice; always mix it with another juice (page 117 and 123). **Buying and storing:** Buy crisp heads with leaves as dark as possible for the specific variety of lettuce. After soaking lettuce in a biodegradable produce wash, or rinsing it under cold water if it is organically grown, spin-dry the leaves. When it is completely dry, store lettuce in large Ziploc plastic bags in the refrigerator for up to a week.

Onions. Onions are extremely strong-tasting and I advise juicing them in small quantities by dropping a few pieces of onion into the hopper and following them with other vegetables. This method rids the juicer of the taste of onion. A little onion juice goes a long way to adding nice, sharp flavor to vegetable juices, just as it adds good flavor to salads.

Onions are related to garlic and have many of the same therapeutic properties. Read the section on garlic to learn more about these. An onion's pungency is caused by essential oils, which normalize the sympathetic nervous system and stimulate beneficial bacteria. Onion juice may also be helpful in expelling mucus from the body. **Buying and storing:** Buy onions with dry, rustling, papery skins free of greenish sunburn spots. The onions should not have "necks." Store them in a cool, dry place away from potatoes. Onions and potatoes react with each other and the onions will soften from absorbed moisture released by the potatoes. Unpeeled onions should not be refrigerated.

Parsley. If you think of parsley as nothing more than a silly little garnish next to an omelet or chicken breast, you could not be further off base. I say eat the parsley and send the omelet and chicken back to the kitchen.

This green leafy vegetable (some people categorize it as an herb) is one of the most nutritious foods in the world. Ancient Greeks and Romans recognized its qualities, using it ritually and medicinally: The Greeks made wreaths of parsley to crown the winners of athletic games; Romans applied it to surface wounds. Today I recommend a poultice made from finely chopped parsley held on a boil or cyst with a clean bandage as a way to draw out toxins and purify the lesion.

The high incidence of chlorophyll in parsley juice metabolizes oxygen in the bloodstream, purifying it and at the same time may act to cleanse the kidneys, liver, and urinary tract. This calms digestive upsets while stimulating digestive enzymes to do their job. It also stimulates the peristaltic wave in the intestines and moves the bowel. Parsley is an excellent source of provitamin A (beta carotene), making it beneficial to eyesight, the capillary system, the adrenal gland, and the thyroid. It is also rich in potassium, sulfur, calcium, magnesium, and chlorine.

Parsley juice is a green juice and should never be drunk by itself or in quantities of more than one or two ounces. One of my favorite daily juices is a combination of carrot, apple, and parsley (page 129). **Buying and storing:** Parsley is easy to find year-round in the greengrocers and supermarkets. Both flat and curly parsley have the same nutritious properties. When you buy it, make sure it is dark green and not yellowing or wilting. Store washed and thoroughly dried parsley in Ziploc bags in the refrigerator. Hardy parsley is easy to grow in the backyard garden patch, ensuring a fresh, organically grown crop for much of the year.

Potatoes. From Malibu to Moscow, Westerners eat potatoes in astounding numbers. This tuber has sustained entire populations in times of famine and in so doing has proved itself a nutritional champ over and over again. Potatoes are one of the nightshade family that, along with tomatoes and peppers, were brought from the New World to the Old by the Spaniards. They quickly became a staple of Northern European diets as well as one of ours.

A medium-size potato supplies a third of the RDA of vitamin C and ranks just below citrus fruits as an important source of that vital vitamin. Potatoes are approximately 20 percent carbohydrates and relatively low in calories (about one hundred in a medium-size tuber). They also supply protein, vitamin B complex, potassium, calcium, and iron. Nearly all the nutrients are on or near the skin.

I do not find potato juice very tasty by itself. I mix it with carrots and apples and sometimes add some parsley and/or watercress for additional flavor (see pages 128 and 135.) **Buying and storing:** I buy big russet potatoes for juicing and baking. I also look for potatoes with eyes. The eyes indicate that the vegetable is capable of sprouting and therefore is full of enzymes and life structure. Potatoes that do not sprout are hybrids or mutants—not my choice for food. But I avoid potatoes that have black spots. Old or improperly stored potatoes develop green tinted skin caused by a toxic alkaloid called solanine. Never buy these, and if the potatoes you have at home look green, toss them out or at least cut away the green parts. Store potatoes in a cool, dry place away from onions. Despite their legendary staying power in root cellars of yesteryear, the potatoes you buy in the markets have been dug up quite some time ago and will keep for only a week or so. Buy only as many as you will use in that time.

Radishes. For all who admire the sharp bite of a radish, it will come as no surprise that radish juice is strong tasting and should not be consumed unless mixed with another vegetable juice. I generally rely on my old standbys, apple and carrot juice.

A small measure of radish juice mixed with a more palatable juice will restore and strengthen mucus membranes, clear sinus cavities, and soothe sore throats. Although nearly 95 percent water, radishes contain significant amounts of potassium, sodium, magnesium, and a small amount of vitamin C. **Buying and storing:** Most radishes sold in the United States are small red orbs with pointed tips. Japanese radishes, called daikon, are long white vegetables resembling a broad white carrot. Both have bold flavor and when purchased should be firm and crisp. Radishes often have the greens attached. This signifies freshness, but cut the tops as soon as you can as they draw nutrients from the root. Store cleaned and dried radishes in the refrigerator for a week or so.

Spinach. Popeye the Sailor Man contributed to the popularity of spinach, but so did the good taste of this iron-rich, dark green, leafy vegetable. Today, Americans are eating an increasing amount of spinach. In the 1970s when cafés and small restaurants began putting a number of salads on their menus, spinach salad led the group. I often order spinach salad when I eat out, requesting that the eggs and bacon be left out. I dress the salad with a squeeze of lemon juice or with organic apple cider vinegar I carry with me.

Raw spinach in salad provides wonderful fiber, but when juiced you get the full benefits of its nutritive properties. Spin-

...ach is a rich source of provitamin A and vitamin C as well as iron. Spinach also has more protein than other leafy vegetables. For cleansing and regenerating the intestinal tract, raw spinach is indispensable. It stimulates the peristaltic wave in the intestines and thus promotes regularity—especially when combined with carrot juice. It also stimulates the liver and lymph glands as well as blood circulation. Spinach is a green juice and so should always be combined with other vegetable juices. **Buying and storing:** Look for crisp, bright green leaves and short stems. Soak spinach leaves in a biodegradable produce wash and then for a while longer in a sinkful of cold water to remove the sand and grit. Rinse the spinach well, spin-dry, and when it is completely dry, store it in large plastic Ziploc bags in the refrigerator for a few days. Spinach turns slimy sooner than lettuce does.

Sprouts. Sprouts are a terrific source of nutrition. I eat them in salads and by themselves to nourish my body with many of the same things that are found in grains and greens. I also juice sprouts to make, for example, the Hair Growth and Hair-Loss Prevention Tonic (page 126). Sprouts are easy to digest—bean sprouts, for example, are certainly easier on the system than the developed bean—and are rich in vitamin C, many minerals, and protein.

There are a number of different kinds of sprouts, from adzuki and alfalfa to sesame and sunflower. Many are common staples in supermarkets while others are found only in natural food stores. Sprouts are very easy to grow and because they should be eaten regularly, it behooves you to grow them yourself in sprouting jars. Get the kids involved—they will love to do it.

Growing Sprouts

Equipment. You need several sprouting jars with perforated lids. These are available in health food stores (for more information on sprouting jars, see page 42).

Method. Put ½ cup of dried legumes, seeds, or grains in a sprouting jar and add distilled water to cover. Soak for 5 to 12 hours (see the chart on page 199 for soaking times).

Drain the water from the jar and put the jar in a dark place such as a cool kitchen cupboard. Rinse the legumes, seeds, or grains every 12 hours, always returning them, drained, to the dark cupboard. When they begin to sprout, to develop "tails" of greenery, place the jar in the sun so that the sprouts develop chlorophyll (see the chart for the number of days required for sprouting).

Grain and legume sprouts are ready for eating when a little green appears. Seeds require more greenery, about 1 to 1½ inches.

Caution: Old legumes, seeds, and grains will not sprout. Discard any that you think are past their time.

String beans. You may be surprised to find string beans among the list of vegetables that take well to juicing. I do not recommend juicing beans by themselves; the juice is unpleasantly thick.

Like all green juices, this can't be consumed alone. I suggest tempering this juice with the sweetness of carrot and/or apple juice.

String beans are rich in calcium, magnesium, phosphorus, and potassium, and contain some protein. They are a

Sprouts

Soaking and Sprouting Chart

Legumes (Beans/Peas)	Soaking Time (hours)	Sprouting Time (days)
Adzuki	9–12	2–3
Garbanzo	10–12	2–3
Lentil	10–12	2–3
Mung	10–12	2–3
Pea	10–12	2–3

Seeds		
Radish	5–8	3–5
Sesame	8–10	3
Sunflower	5–8	2–3

Grains		
Alfalfa	5–8	3–5
Corn	12–15	3–5
Millet	8–10	1–2
Rice	10–12	3–4
Rye	10–12	2–3
Triticale	10–12	2–3
Wheatgrass	10–12	7–9

good source of the vitamin B complex as well as bioflavonoids for strengthening capillaries and blood vessels. **Buying and storing:** Fresh string beans should break with a noticeable snap. Never buy flabby beans. Soak them in a biodegradable produce wash, and when they are dry, store them in the refrigerator for several days.

Sweet potatoes. In the United States, we call potatolike vegetables with dark orange, exceptionally moist flesh "yams," and drier tubers with lighter-colored flesh "sweet potatoes." In fact all are sweet potatoes, but who is arguing? I prefer yams, as darker color means higher vitamin content.

Sweet potatoes are among the best sources of beta carotene in the vegetable world, rivaling broccoli and carrots. They are also rich in vitamin C, calcium, potassium, carbohydrates, and fiber. In fact, sweet potatoes are as close to perfect as a single food can be. People have been known to subsist on them alone with little or no known vitamin or mineral deprivation. (For the value of beta carotene and other nutrients, see the sections on broccoli and carrots in this chapter.) Mixing carrot and sweet potato juice is also extremely beneficial to the complexion. **Buying and storing:** Buy plump sweet potatoes that are firm, medium-size, and taper at the ends. Their color should be good and the skin smooth without cuts and bruises. Store sweet potatoes in a cool place for about a week.

Swiss chard. Treat Swiss chard as you would a green. It is a form of beet grown for its greenery and not its root. Chard is a source of iron and provitamin A and vitamin C. You must mix chard juice with other juices, especially carrot and apple. **Buying and storing:** Choose chard that is very fresh with no yellow or brown portions on the leaves. Coarse, large stalks indicate the chard will be woody and pithy—smaller chard is more tender. After washing it, store chard in the refrigerator in plastic bags for a few days. Juice it as soon as possible for its full benefits.

Tomatoes. Botanically speaking, tomatoes are fruit, but because most of us think of them as vegetables, I am grouping them here. However, consider a tomato as you would a melon and do not combine it with other juice. Follow my rule for melons: "Use it alone or leave it alone." However, nearly every rule has an exception to prove it, and the exception here is celery and cucumber juice. A little of both or either added to tomato juice makes a very fine drink (page 131).

When you juice fresh, ripe, juicy tomatoes, do not expect the syrupy, salty liquid that pours from a can. Fresh tomato juice is thick and cloudy and tastes far more of the tomato than canned does. Canned tomato juice is cooked, distilled, filtered, and often salted.

Eaten raw and preferably right from the vine, tomatoes provide the body with sulfur, phosphorus, and organic sodium. The vitamin C content of a tomato is more than 50 percent of the recommended daily allowance. **Buying and storing:** The best tomatoes are well shaped with a distinctive aroma. Their color is deep red, although they may be yellow at the stem end. They feel heavy and yielding when pressed. Whenever possible buy locally grown, vine-ripened tomatoes. If they are grown organically, all the better, as these have the best flavor. Few people will dispute that just-picked summer tomatoes are among the greatest treats from the garden. Green tomatoes should be avoided, as they may be harmful to the kidneys. The tomatoes that you buy in the market may be red but probably were picked green and gassed so that they turned red. This does not always mean they are ripe—and it rarely means they taste good. Let overly firm tomatoes sit out at room temperature for four or five days.

They will ripen further and soften. Otherwise, store tomatoes for a few days in the refrigerator or in a cool area. They do not keep very long once they are completely ripe.

Watercress. Peppery watercress livens up raw salads and it also makes a valuable juice. Watercress juice is a green juice and must not be consumed alone. It also tastes bitter and is much easier to swallow if mixed with carrot, potato, and a little parsley (page 135) or carrot, spinach, and turnip leaves (page 104). **Buying and storing:** Watercress is increasingly available in supermarkets and greengrocers. Buy fresh-looking greens with springy leaves that show no evidence of wilting and yellowing. Soak watercress in a biodegradable produce wash unless it is organically grown, in which case simply rinse it in cold water and dry it. Store it in large plastic Ziploc bags in the refrigerator for two or three days.

Wheatgrass. Wheatgrass is a super source of chlorophyll and also has the widest range of vitamins and minerals of any of the vegetables I've described in this chapter. The hitch to this is that wheatgrass is not readily available to the everyday consumer.

I attribute Dr. Ann Wigmore of Hippocrates Health Institute, an expert in the field of living foods nutrition, with pioneering the research to establish the value of wheatgrass. She found that wheatgrass juice duplicates the molecular structure of hemoglobin, a vital part of the blood, and because it is so rich in free-radical scavengers provided by its high incidence of provitamin A, it may inhibit malignancies. The chlorophyll it contains is a cell stimulator, rejuvenator, and red blood cell builder. It also purifies the blood which helps to cleanse the kidneys, liver, and urinary tract. This contributes to regularity and a healthy bowel.

You probably have never considered ingesting wheatgrass, and to be honest, I never had either until I met a fellow by the name of LeClaire in St. Petersburg, Florida. This was back in the 1950s and Mr. LeClaire came to a juicing demonstration even though he shook so much from Parkinson's disease he could not hold a cup and sample any of the juices. Nevertheless he bought a juicer. The next year when I returned to Florida, Mr. LeClaire approached the front of the room and shook my hand without trembling. I was amazed. He explained that he had put himself on a regimen of carrot juice, wheatgrass juice, and leafy greens. Wheatgrass juice was the centerpiece of his diet and he consumed six ounces every day. Fascinated, I accepted his invitation to his rooming house to see how he grew wheatgrass in trays, using carrot and leafy green waste for compost and growing worms to aerate the soil in five-gallon, stainless steel milk cans. Since that day, I have believed as strongly as anyone in the power of wheatgrass. Linda and I grow it by the trayful at home and make sure we drink it regularly combined with carrot and/or apple juice (page 95). Consumed by itself it is extremely sweet and may make you nauseated. Never drink more than two ounces at one time. **Buying and storing:** If you cannot find wheatgrass in markets or at farm stands, you can grown your own. All you need is the room and the desire to do something really good for yourself and your family. Whole winter wheat berries are sold in bulk in health food stores.

Growing Wheatgrass

Equipment

2 14- by 18-inch metal or plastic cafeteria trays (available at restaurant supply houses) or similar trays

50-50 mixture of topsoil and peat moss (both available at garden centers and nurseries)

2 large plastic trash containers with tight-fitting lids, reserved exclusively for this project

Method.

Drill holes 4 inches apart around the circumference of the sides of one of the trash containers for ventilation. This one will be used for wheatgrass compost. Store the soil–peat moss mixture in the other container.

Soak 1 cup of whole winter wheat berries in water to cover for 12 hours. Pour off the water and let the berries drain for another 12 hours. Rinse the berries two to three times during this period to prevent them from drying out.

Fill one tray with the soil–peat moss mixture and spread it evenly to a depth of 1 inch. Spray or sprinkle the soil with water to dampen it thoroughly. Do not soak the soil.

Spread the drained wheat berries evenly over the soil. Cover the planted tray with the second tray upside down. Leave the covered tray alone for three days.

On the fourth day, lift off the top tray and water the sprouting wheatgrass. Set the uncovered tray in sunlight, if possible, and water it once a day for three days. On the seventh day the grass will be 3 or 4 inches high and ready for harvesting.

Harvest the wheatgrass with scissors or a sharp knife by cutting it as close to the roots as possible. The sprouted grass will keep for days if you make 2 or 3 ounces of juice a day. Keep the grasses watered.

When the wheatgrass is harvested, break the matted soil

into pieces and put them in the compost container. Continue to add pieces of soil and other waste from the juicer. After three months or so the mats will have broken down and be ready to reuse as soil. Turn the compost from time to time. Dampen and mix the new soil with peat moss, but in a mixture of 75 percent soil and 25 percent peat moss. Use this to plant more wheat berries or use in the garden as you would any compost.

Notes: To ensure that you always have wheatgrass for juicing, buy three trays so one is in the initial stage of cultivation and the other in the end stage. The third tray is the cover, needed only for three days of each cycle.

The compost container should contain mostly wheatgrass mats if it is to be used again for growing wheatgrass. This will ensure that the soil is rich in nutrients. You might also choose to have two compost containers in operation during the first few months so that the contents of one has time to break down while you are filling the other. After a while, one will meet your needs. Keep the compost outside or in the garage.

Zucchini. I juice squash in the summertime when it is young and plentiful. Similar in nutritional content to cucumbers, zucchini acts as a natural coolant and thirst quencher, replenishing the body with needed fluids. As it does this, it also acts as an internal cleanser (see note on page 100). The juice is bland and should be mixed with carrots or apples. **Buying and storing:** Large zucchini has tough skin and dry flesh. Buy it when it is small and tender. Store zucchini in the refrigerator for a few days. You will get the most nutrients if you juice it shortly after buying it.

6

Vitamins, Minerals, and the Importance of Fiber

Vitamins and minerals are essential to life. Without them, the body fails to metabolize and grow normally and is susceptible to disease. Luckily, sufficient vitamins and minerals are readily available in fruits, vegetables, grains, and legumes. When the fruits and vegetables are consumed as juice, the vitamins and minerals are quickly released into the bloodstream and race directly to the cells requiring them most. Every minute of every day, your body works long and hard sorting and utilizing vitamins and minerals to keep you functioning and healthy. When you deprive your body of necessary nutrients it has to compensate by drawing them from other parts of the body. Eventually, this causes illness.

When we eat whole foods, the body goes into action. It becomes the ultimate juicer, extracting what it needs from the food and converting it into liquid. The juice diet not only supplies the body with the vitamins and minerals it needs but permits it to skip a step in the digestive process by juicing the food for us. This helps the body benefit nutritionally at a fantastic rate. When we drink juice, our food is already in a liquid state. Nutrients are absorbed quickly and go right to work.

These are pure and natural nutrients, derived directly from live foods as nature made them. No food scientist, biochemist, lab technician, or food packager has fiddled with them. Only the sun, the soil, and the rain have conspired to deliver the life-giving nutrients to you in the form of luscious fruits and vegetables.

To grasp how valuable fruits and vegetables are to your everyday and lifelong health, it is helpful to understand the powers of the different vitamins and minerals naturally within them. What follows is not a dense scientific tract but a clear, concise discussion of precisely what I find most beneficial about vitamins and minerals.

Vitamins

Vitamins fall into two categories: fat-soluble and water-soluble. Fat-soluble vitamins are stored in the body and utilized as needed. Water-soluble vitamins are not stored and must be replenished every day. Vitamins A, D, E, and K are fat-soluble; the vitamin B complex and vitamin C are water-soluble.

Fat-Soluble Vitamins

Vitamin A. When referring to vitamin A, I often use the term "provitamin A," which means, in a sense, previtamin. Provitamin A is the agent in fruits and vegetables that is also known as beta carotene. When beta carotene is consumed, the body converts it into vitamin A. Not a vegetable or fruit in the world actually contains "vitamin A," but a good number of them have provitamin A or beta carotene, also called carotenoid. Confusing? Don't worry about it; rest assured that juicing ensures that you absorb a lot of beta carotene. For example, simply by drinking carrot juice, you are getting a terrific amount.

Provitamin A derived from vegetables and fruit is so safe you cannot overdose on it. Your body will get "too much" vitamin A only if you supplement your diet with fish oil capsules. Such overdosing can be toxic and can cause adverse symptoms—but you do not need to worry. It's impossible to OD when you absorb beta carotene in its natural state: fresh fruits and vegetables.

Vitamin A contributes to a strong immune system, improves vision, and helps protect against cancer of the lungs, larynx, esophagus, and bladder. Some evidence points to its being the agent that reduces the tendency of malignant cells to multiply. It prevents a host of skin diseases and combats the effects of aging.

As well as other juices, I drink a lot of carrot juice for vitamin A. A fifty-fifty mixture of carrot and apple juice is one of the greatest drinks in the world. During the summer when apricots and cantaloupe are readily available and deliciously ripe I juice them for their terrific taste and excellent measures of provitamin A. Other sources are broccoli, spinach, squash, sweet potatoes, beet greens, peaches, tomatoes, watermelon, kale, cabbage, and cauliflower. The list goes on!

Vitamin D. This vitamin is produced by the skin when it is exposed to sunlight. Drinking juices from foods rich in beta carotene (see vitamin A), especially carrot juice, helps protect you from the harmful rays of the sun (but don't neglect the sun block), which is good news. This means you can spend time outdoors exercising, gardening, sketching, etc., and producing vitamin D.

Vitamin D promotes strong bones and teeth by aiding in the absorption of calcium, a process that continues well into our later years and makes vitamin D important for senior citizens. A loss of vitamin D can contribute to bone fractures and rheumatism in older people caused by a condition called osteomalacia. And vitamin D deficiency, rare in the United States, is a leading cause of rickets.

So, please, take a walk or sit on a park bench and let the sun shine on you!

Vitamin E. As an antioxidant, vitamin E guards against cardiovascular and neurological disorders. It allows fewer cells to be harmed when blood vessels have been cut, mangled, or burned and so is valuable for healing wounds and preventing scarring. It helps keep the heart muscle lubricated. It contributes to virility and protects against sterility in men. It also protects the body against some effects of air pollution.

I get my vitamin E mainly from the carrot juice I voraciously consume each day. You also will find vitamin E in whole grain cereals, beets, celery, leafy greens, and vegetables.

Vitamin K. Found in a wide range of foods, vitamin K aids in coagulation of the blood and mineralization of the bones. It was named by Henrik Dam, a Danish biochemist who suggested calling it *Koagulations* after its very important function. But that term was shortened to vitamin K. Vitamin K helps fractures heal successfully and may also have a role in preventing osteoporosis. There is also evidence that vitamin K may reduce the chance of some cancers such as lung, ovarian, and breast.

Deficiencies of vitamin K are extremely rare and our bodies need to absorb it along with other vitamins during our entire life. Newborn babies are vitamin K deficient and may have blood-clotting problems in their first few days of life. Sometimes antibiotic therapy can deplete the body of vitamin K. Eat and juice a good supply of dark leafy greens to maintain a good supply of it.

Water-Soluble Vitamins

Vitamin B complex. The vitamin B complex includes B_1 (thiamine), B_2 (riboflavin), B_3 (niacin), B_6 (pyridoxine), B_{12} (cobalamin), and folic acid, pantothenic acid, and biotin. Also included are the chemical substances choline, inositol, PABA (para-aminobenzoic acid), pangamic acid, laetrile, and orotic acid.

The B complex works in combination to nurture and heal the entire body. All its elements are synergistic and intertwined. While the complex has many functions, perhaps its most vital is metabolizing carbohydrates, fats, and proteins. This is responsible for much of our energy, athletic performance, healthy skin, and toxic-free systems, and for retarding hair loss and preventing early graying. A great source of the

B complex is leafy greens and sprouts, especially alfalfa sprouts and wheatgrass.

Vitamin B₁ (thiamine) is important because it converts blood sugar into energy. It is also key in maintaining a healthy heart and helps control diabetes. Research indicates it keeps us mentally alert and neurologically healthy. It is important, too, in the treatment of anemia.

Since alcohol intake interfers with thiamine more than with any other nutrient, thiamine can become the most commonly deficient vitamin in the B complex. Serious thiamine deficiency is called beriberi. Beriberi is characterized by mental confusion, blurred vision, and a staggering gait. In its most critical stages, it results in heart failure.

Vitamin B₁ is found in all plant life and most plentifully in whole grains, brown rice, beans, sprouts, and legumes.

Vitamin B₂ (riboflavin) helps metabolize energy and is especially beneficial to anyone who exercises strenuously as it also increases performance. It is credited with protecting against anemia and some cancers. Similar to thiamine's, riboflavin's deficiency occurs most frequently in diabetics and often dietrestricted individuals. B₂ deficiency is indicated by cracking skin at the corners of the mouth and lips, light-sensitive eyes, and eczema. Riboflavin is available in green leafy vegetables, sprouts, and cereals.

Vitamin B₃ (niacin) lowers cholesterol and protects against cardiovascular disease and high blood pressure. It also flushes the system of pollutants from the air and the systems of those who use tobacco and alcohol. Niacin plays a role in relieving migraines and the symptoms of arthritis and is available in leafy greens, sprouts, and grains.

Vitamins B₆ and B₁₂ (pyridoxine and cobalamin), both part of the B complex, respectively help boost the immune system and energize us. B₆ is available in whole grains, but B₁₂ is a little harder to come by. Many nutritionists say the only sources are animal products, but you can get sufficient B₁₂—and you need only minuscule amounts—in nutritional yeast and fermented food like tempeh, a traditional Asian staple.

The rest of the components of the B complex are readily available in leafy greens and it is extremely rare for anyone to suffer from a deficiency of any of these.

Vitamin C (ascorbic acid). This is perhaps the best-known vitamin. It acts as an antiseptic maintaining tissues, joints, and ligaments against inflammation. It protects against tenderness and bleeding of the gums. It fights colds and flu. Recent studies indicate that vitamin C may help prevent gastric and esophageal cancer.

Almost everyone knows vitamin C is good for the body, yet a staggering number of adults in the United States are deficient in it. Why? Because they do not eat enough leafy greens and fresh fruits, believing perhaps that a small glass of orange juice from concentrate is all they need.

Juicing leafy greens and citrus fruit is the best way to ensure that you get enough vitamin C. Juicing introduces all the components of the vitamin, including bioflavonoids that live in the white pulpy parts of citrus fruits and the ribs of bell peppers as well as in green leafy vegetables.

Although not a vitamin, bioflavonoids are sometimes called vitamin P. Albert Szent-Györgyi, whose discovery of vitamin C was one of the many lifetime achievements that earned him the Nobel Prize in medicine, also identified bioflavonoids and suggested calling them vitamin P. Working in tandem with vitamin C, bioflavonoids have antiviral properties, contribute to healthy capillaries, and prevent disorders such as gum bleeding.

Some of the best sources of vitamin C are broccoli, cauliflower, potatoes, tomatoes, Brussels sprouts, apples, citrus fruits, green and red bell peppers, and strawberries.

Minerals

Humans cannot assimilate minerals unless they first are processed through plants, and the best way to do this is by eating a lot of vegetables and fruits—or better yet, by juicing a lot of vegetables and fruits. What follows is a glossary of most of the essential minerals and trace elements that, if you eat a balanced diet of whole foods, fresh fruits and vegetables, and nutrient-rich juices, your body will never be without.

Calcium. One of the most essential minerals, calcium is particularly important for growing children and women. A number of postmenopausal women are susceptible to a condition called osteoporosis, a crippling disease that is manifested by stooped posture and often a humped back and that has been linked to calcium deficiency. The dairy industry tells us to eat more cheese and drink lots of milk for the calcium. I say, juice your vegetables.

Plant foods have supplied many nondairy-consuming cultures with calcium for centuries. Calcium-rich vegetables include kale, parsley, and broccoli. (Remember to mix green juices such as broccoli and kale juice with another juice such as apple or carrot juice in a 1:4 ratio.) Other calcium-rich foods include sesame and sunflower seeds, seaweed, almonds, molasses, and brewer's yeast.

Most of the calcium the average adult carries in him is constantly being reabsorbed into the bloodstream and reused. Therefore, it is imperative that we regularly replace the calcium that ebbs and flows from our bones throughout life.

Besides calcium building strong bones, it also helps regulate the heartbeat and aids blood clotting. And it stimulates enzyme activity for digestion of fat and protein.

I cannot emphasize enough how important calcium is. Drink calcium-rich juices regularly. Eating the same foods does not supply nearly enough of the mineral. As well as the leafy greens I've already mentioned, try juicing sprouts, watercress, mint leaves (I really like spearmint-apple juice) wheatgrass, and barley greens.

Copper. Copper is crucial for the proper absorption of iron in the body (see the section on iron) and thus thorough blood oxygenation. Too much copper can be harmful, which is why it is inadvisable to cook in unlined copper pans. If you get copper by drinking fresh juices and eating lots of greens, there is no danger of overdosing on it. I suggest potato-carrot juices (pages 128 and 135) and Swiss chard-carrot juice (page 117).

Iodine. In landlocked regions of a country miles from the sea, the absence of iodine in the soil used to be a major problem, as the deficiency of this in the diet caused goiters. Today, the condition is practically nonexistent in the United States and other developed countries since we have learned how important the tiny amount of iodine we need actually is. Iodine is essential to healthy thyroid activity and consequently our general well-being. It also clears mucus from breathing tubes and is a good antiseptic. Iodine is often added to table salt to ensure that everyone gets the small amount necessary to good health. You can also get iodine in radishes and wheatgrass juice. Be sure to juice these to get the maximum food value and absorb the iodine you need.

Iron. Iron reoxygenates red blood cells by building up hemoglobin to carry oxygen to every cell in the body; this is particularly vital for the cells in the brain so we stay mentally alert and those in the lungs so our respiratory system stays in good working order. Iron also keeps our energy level up and stimulates the immune system. It prevents internal cells from premature atrophy. Iron deficiency causes anemia, a condition that results in fatigue, skin pallor, and in some cases irritability and mental lethargy. Severe anemia results in breathing difficulties.

Although all people require iron for good health, women and children are most likely to be anemic. Pregnant women in particular need a lot of iron.

I get much of my iron from apricots, one of my favorite fruits. When I cannot juice apricots, I eat them dried and always carry a package with me for quick snacking. Other excellent sources of iron are leafy greens such as spinach and certain nuts. Have you tried spinach-carrot juice (page 124) yet? A top-notch drink for good health. Or how about greens-carrot-apple juice (pages 116 and 101)?

Magnesium. Along with potassium, magnesium is present in nearly every cell of the body and is vital to its functioning. It is important for muscle action, for the metabolism of food, and, working with calcium, for strong bones and bone marrow. It also works to keep the nervous system operating on an even keel and plays an important role in the proper functioning of the heart.

As necessary as magnesium is, a number of people have a minor magnesium deficiency. Those at risk are the elderly, dieters, diabetics, anyone taking diuretics, heavy drinkers, pregnant women, and athletes. Luckily, magnesium is readily available in leafy greens. Some of the best juices for ensuring proper levels of magnesium are carrot–apple–beet (page 143), carrot–broccoli (page 103), and carrot–Brussels sprouts (page 138).

Manganese. There has not been much research done on the role of manganese in human health but what we do know convinces science that the mineral is vital to good health. It plays a role in normal brain functioning, bone development, reproductive health, and glucose metabolism. As a component of the antioxidant enzyme, it scavenges free-radicals and promotes cell health. It is nearly impossible to ingest more than you can tolerate, although mine workers who are exposed to the mineral's dust have been known to suffer from "manganese madness"—a degenerative disease that has similar symptoms to Parkinson's disease. Manganese deficiency, on the other hand, may lead to decreased antibody production and/or secretion.

Nature ensures that we do not absorb too much or too little manganese if we eat a balanced diet. The best sources for this mineral are nuts, whole grains, split peas, spinach, raisins, beet greens, Brussels sprouts, carrots, broccoli, corn, cabbage, and gingerroot.

Phosphorus. Working with calcium, phosphorus builds strong bones and teeth. Part of its job is to strengthen hair, fingernails, and cuticles; another part is to absorb fat properly. It also counters fatigue, regulates the body's internal thermostat, and affects its energy level. Phosphorus feeds the brain, particularly the hypothalamus. I suggest cauliflower–carrot-parsley juice (page 113) for phosphorus.

Potassium. This mineral is not hard to find in any number of fruits, vegetables, and grains, and it is absolutely essential to life. The problem lies in consuming too much sodium in the form of table salt and disturbing the all-important sodium-potassium balance in the body. In other words, as we increase our intake of salt, we should also increase our intake of potassium, something few people do. But there is an easier way to achieve the balance. Decrease salt intake (see the section on sodium).

The perfect balance of potassium and sodium that our body works so hard to maintain stimulates and regulates the heartbeat, eliminates edema, tightens the collagen in the skin so that the skin looks healthier and smoother, maintains weight, and relieves muscle cramps. Most important, this balance seems to be directly related to controlling hypertension and strokes.

Dr. Norman W. Walker, who taught me so much over the years, told me about the most efficient way to get potassium into the body. He called it "raw potassium broth," and while the name may not sound very appetizing, it is delicious and does wonders for your health. My version for this is carrot-celery-spinach-parsley juice (page 125). Another excellent potassium drink is apple-celery juice (page 150).

Selenium. This important trace element is getting increasing attention as a cancer fighter and guard against heart disease. It also reduces the inflammation caused by arthritis and increases fertility. Last but not least, selenium plays a major role in counteracting the free radicals of aging cells so that the skin looks more youthful and elastic. It is a great anti-aging mineral.

I get selenium from garlic, cabbage, and broccoli, among

other vegetables. And my carrot-celery-parsley-garlic juice (page 130) is sure to be your very own fountain of youth.

Silicon. Do you remember the smooth, elastic skin of youth? Make sure you get enough silicon in your diet and your skin will look better than ever: unblemished, unwrinkled, and firm. Silicon is terrific for remedying brittle fingernails and keeping your hair from turning gray prematurely. And it is also fantastic for relieving the pain of tendinitis and related inflammation and soreness in the tendons and ligaments. All greens are good sources of silicon, but I especially urge you to try green bell peppers mixed with carrot juice (page 98) and the AAA Juice (page 95).

Sodium. Approximately 70 percent of the earth's surface is covered with water, all but a fraction being salt water. Our bodies reflect the same makeup, being nearly 70 percent salt water. Natural, organic sodium is essential to life. A balance of potassium and sodium keeps the body functioning perfectly, aids digestion, regulates carbon dioxide levels, prevents fluid retention, and allows the heart to operate at a normal rate. The sodium helps prevent muscle cramping and fatigue.

When I say sodium I do not mean inorganic sodium chloride. That is table salt, the white stuff from the salt mines we grind and sift and put in salt shakers. Too much of it, especially when it knocks out the potassium-sodium balance, causes kidney and bladder problems, hypertension, and heart disease. No one disputes that most of us consume too much salt—as much as ten to twenty times as much as we really need. By eating vegetables such as spinach and celery that have naturally converted inorganic sodium from the soil into organic sodium our bodies absorb sufficient sodium. With a balanced, healthful diet, there's no need to sprinkle salt on anything ever again.

Sulfur. Sulfur purifies our intestinal walls and is important for liver metabolism. It is an element of insulin and contributes to the health of cartilage, bones, teeth, fingernails, and hair. Cabbage, kale, garlic, and onions are all good sources of sulfur. Drink cabbage juice (a quarter cabbage, the rest carrot, celery, or apple) and juices containing small amounts of garlic and onion.

Zinc. Zinc protects the immune system, which is without doubt its most vital function. It also helps prevent some age-related blindness and keeps the senses—taste and smell—in good order too. Often, impotent males are helped by zinc. It is used in some capacity to treat infertility problems and those of the prostate. Zinc also is useful for treating acne. Make sure you absorb all the zinc you need by drinking juices made from leafy greens, gingerroot, and cruciferous vegetables. Two terrific zinc drinks are carrot-parsley juice (page 130) and carrot-apple-ginger-parsley juice (page 116).

Fiber

I have said it before and I will say it again. I consider myself a fruitarian when I eat, a vegetarian when I juice. Why? Because every day the body needs to absorb a good supply of the life-giving nutrients you have just read about. The best way to do this is by juicing foods rich in these all-important vitamins and minerals and then eating around the juice to get enough dietary fiber. Vegetables are the body builders; fruits are the energizers and cleansers. Fruits don't take as long to digest as vegetables—only about twenty minutes—and even eaten whole are very easy on the system. Fruit also is a terrific source of fiber. Just as we need vitamins and minerals each day of our lives, we also need fiber.

Our bodies are the optimal juicers, extracting all the vitamins and minerals they need in liquid form from the food we eat. What is left after the liquid is "juiced" is fiber. It is the juice of the fiber that feeds us.

The fiber moves from the stomach into the intestines and then is eliminated through the bowel. But fiber has more value than simply acting as a vessel for nutrients which is then expelled when no longer needed. It exercises the gums, stimulates peristalsis, cleans the colon, and helps us absorb vitamin D.

As most of us know, constipation is uncomfortable, debilitating, and can lead to more serious ailments. Consuming a good amount of fiber helps with regularity. But fiber does even more. The American Cancer Society explains that studies "seem to support an association between high-fiber diets and low incidence of cancer and other diseases of the colon. The exact mechanism is not known but could be related to dilution of intestinal contents and speeding up their passage through the colon." Its literature advises that we eat more bran and cereals and recommends reading the labels of everything we buy that we believe to be high in fiber. For instance, the first ingredient on the label for high-fiber bread should be a whole grain flour, such as whole wheat.

We hear a lot about the value of fiber in the press, on television, from our doctors, and from our friends. Everyone tells us to eat more fiber. I say, eat a diet that is at least 50 percent raw and you will get all the fiber you need. What is more, in its recommendations for increasing the amount of fiber in the diet, the American Cancer Society puts forth practices I have been advocating for years. It says to leave the skins on potatoes, fruits, and vegetables; eat whole fruit for breakfast; eat a good amount of legumes such as beans and lentils. The foods listed in its literature on fiber sound like a litany of my favorite fruits and vegetables: apricots, prunes, figs, dried beans, corn, peas, spinach, sweet potatoes, potatoes, Brussels sprouts, blueberries, dates, raisins, apples, pears, and oranges.

The fruits I enjoy eating the most for fiber are bananas, pears, and strawberries. I would like everyone to start the day with a piece of whole fruit. Let's face it, eating several pieces of fruit through the day is more palatable and easier than eating a plateful of parsley or twenty to thirty carrots. I probably have not eaten more than one hundred carrots in my entire life—but I have juiced almost one million. Every now and then I eat a little coleslaw or dip a cucumber slice in vinegar and chew it very well. Otherwise, I get my fiber from fruits, baked potatoes now and then, brown rice, legumes—and more fruits.

7

Juice for What Ails You

*B*y now you are well aware that fresh juices made from healthful fruits and vegetables provide the body with an astounding array of nutrients. Almost before our digestive systems kick in, the nutrients in the juice we drink go to work protecting and strengthening our every living cell. These cells may be in our skin, hair, bones, or teeth. They may be part of our internal organs, heart, or brain. All are synergistically important to good health.

However, as carefully as we try, we are not always in good health. Wintertime and closed rooms bring colds and flu; old sports injuries can flare up as uncomfortable arthritis; our mouths develop painful canker sores; constipation causes gastric distress; weak, aging bones become osteoporotic. Other afflictions interfere with everyday life, too: insomnia, acne, fatigue, headache, tooth decay, bleeding gums, and hair loss. At different times in our lives we may suffer from weight gain, loss of energy, or anxiety. As each birthday passes, we may worry about losing hair and gaining wrinkles. And there are more serious diseases that touch far too many of us, such as heart disease, cancer, and diabetes.

In this chapter I am going to describe the vitamins and minerals and different juices that benefit the body and equip it with the right tools for handling physical problems and disease. I am not promoting miracle cures. There's no magic here. I am offering good old-fashioned, commonsense advice. Eat well, exercise, and get enough sleep, my friends, and you will feel better and live a more healthful life.

I recommend reading Chapter 5, "Fruits and Vegetables—and Why They Are So Good for You" as a companion to this section. This will provide you with a rounded explanation of the benefits of the fruits and vegetables and the juices, plus give you a wider range of juicing ideas for various conditions.

Common Ailments

Common ailments are the everyday irritants of living. Not all of us are affected by every one of them, and those that do plague us do it at different points in our lives. I feel the various fruits and vegetables recommended for juicing help reduce or relieve these common problems or ailments and contribute to a more joyful and energetic life.

Aching bones and tooth problems. Vegetables such as broccoli, kale, and other greens are high in calcium and in other important vitamins and minerals that promote strong bones and teeth. Try the Bone-Building Tonic (page 101), Eye Beautifier Juice (page 120), The Broccoli Cheer (page 103), and any of the juices noted as "calcium drink," such as Green Power (page 125) and Tangerine Sky (page 88).

Acid stomach. Juices noted as "alkaline drinks" help to calm acid stomach, including carrot-cucumber-beet juice (page 100) and carrot-cabbage-celery juice (page 96). Juices containing potato and jicama relieve the distress of acid stomachs. Try potato-carrot-apple-parsley juice (page 128) and jicama-carrot-apple-celery juice (page 133). Juices with watercress in them are good antiacids too. Consider The Bunny Hop (page 104) and Lung Tonic (page 135).

Acne. Juices made from vegetables with a good measure of silicon are helpful for keeping the skin clear of blemishes. Try The Blemish Blaster (page 98) and Idaho Trailblazer (page 128). Juices with watercress may prove beneficial too.

Anxiety. When you feel anxious or nervous, try a glass of grape juice such as the Christmas Cocktail (page 54) or the Passion Cocktail (page 78). Any juice containing strawberries is a smart choice too. In the vegetable kingdom, I suggest juices containing carrots, celery, and even asparagus. Try The Champ (page 114), a classic, and also Calming Nightcap (page 106), and any of the "alkaline juices." Another good juice for nervousness is Waldorf Salad (page 150).

Bleeding gums. Grapefruit juice or any juice containing citrus fruit can be helpful for gum bleeding. Another choice is The Key Wester (page 69).

Bruising. The bioflavonoids in orange juice (page 56) help to strengthen blood vessels and capillaries and hence bruises heal more quickly. Other citrus juices are good for this too.

Canker sores/fever blisters. The quinic acid naturally occurring in cranberries make cranberry juice a good treatment for sores on the mouth and lips. How about Morning Blush (page 74) or The Cape Codder (page 53)?

Colds. You will not be surprised to hear that citrus fruits are among the best for warding off colds. Pineapple and cranberry juices can be helpful too. Since both apple-cranberry juice (page 53) and Cranberry-Grape-Pineapple Juice (page 55) are sweet, refreshing, and delicious, they will taste good on those days you do not feel up to par. Another good tonic for colds is juice containing ginger, which acts as a mucus expectorant. And garlic juice is good for warding off both colds and flu. Drink it in very small amounts and always mix it with other juices; try Jay's Secret (page 130) and Satin Skin Juice (page 145). Juices containing a little ginger or radish juice help to clear sinus cavities and strengthen mucus membranes.

Constipation. Adding more fiber to your diet is, of course, the best way to improve bowel movements. In addition, vegetable juices go a long way toward relieving constipation. Try juices containing asparagus, potatoes, and jicamas. Potato-carrot-apple-parsley juice (page 128) is a good choice. The fruit juice I find works best is apple-pear juice (page 58).

Digestion problems. Apples are among the best digestive aids. Try carrot-apple juice (page 114), apple-pear juice (page 58), Fennel-Apple Juice (page 121), or any other apple drink. The Digestive Cocktail (page 57) made from citrus juice is great too. Another of my favorite juices for good digestion is Cantaloupe Juice (page 52). Garlic stimulates the flow of digestive enzymes and rids the body of toxins through the skin. Consume only small amounts of garlic juice at a time—a little packs a big punch—by trying Jay's Secret (page 130). Remember: Never drink garlic juice by itself.

Eczema. Watercress juice, with its high concentration of sulfur and chlorine, can be beneficial to anyone suffering from eczema. But don't forget to combine this green juice with at least three times the amount of a nongreen juice like carrot. Try The Bunny Hop (page 104) and Lung Tonic (page 135).

Effects of secondhand cigarette smoke and other pollutants. I recommend green leafy vegetables and also strawberry juice for diminishing the pollution collecting in your lungs when you breathe cigarette smoke. Strawberries contain ellagitannin, which is converted by the body into ellagic acid. A recent study by scientists at Case Western Reserve University suggests that ellagic acid may prevent environmental chemicals from converting into cancer-causing substances in the body. This goes for smokers as well as nonsmokers who are exposed to cigarettes. Honolulu-California Connector (page 67) is my favorite strawberry drink. Try The Bunny Hop (page 104) for its leafy greens. Celery juice is beneficial too for cleansing the body of excessive carbon dioxide. Watercress and parsley are great as well: The juice named Lung Tonic (page 135) is delicious and contains both of these.

Fatigue/flagging energy/stamina. Try carrot juice, alone or combined with apple or another kind of juice, especially celery and/or parsley, for a jolt of natural energy and increased stamina. I suggest the Pick-Me-Up Energy Cocktail (page 139), Jay's Secret (page 130), AAA Juice (page 95), Jay's Best (page 129), and especially for athletes before, during, and after strenuous workouts, Green Power (page 125).

It is equally important to get enough magnesium, which contributes directly to stamina and energy levels. Many greens, particularly dandelion greens, are high in magnesium. Try the Zippy Spring Tonic (page 151), for sustaining energy and stamina.

Flu. All the citrus juices are good for relieving the symptoms of flu, but I particularly like creamy orange juice (page 56), and tangerine juice. When I feel the aches and pains of flu coming on, I drink a big glass of cranberry juice right away—and often the symptoms disappear. Both apple-cranberry (page 53) and Cranberry-Grape-Pineapple (page 55) are excellent choices as are juices containing a little ginger or garlic.

Gum disease. Try juices high in magnesium, such as the Zippy Spring Tonic (page 151). Juices high in vitamin C can also be beneficial. Linda's Morning Sunrise (page 71) is an all-time great.

Headaches. The next time your head aches, juice some celery and apples to make Waldorf Salad Juice (page 150) or try any other drink containing celery. Fennel-Apple Juice (page 121) has much the same effect.

Hemorrhoids. The juices recommended in the section on digestion keep your system regular; this helps avoid nasty hemorrhoids. When you suffer from them, try jicama-pear-apple juice (page 144) (jicamas are potatolike vegetables available in Hispanic markets and a growing number of greengrocers, see page 191) and any juice made with potatoes, such as potato-carrot-apple-parsley juice (page 128).

Impotency. Try adding gingerroot to your juices for its high zinc content, a mineral that helps fight impotency. Cruciferous vegetables contain a fair share of selenium, which may increase male potency. Try any juice with cabbage, broccoli, kale, or other cruciferous vegetables.

Many people have told us too that wheatgrass works wonders in this department. One of the best wheatgrass combinations is the AAA Juice (page 95).

Insomnia. Having trouble sleeping? Try a glass of Cantaloupe Juice (page 52) or the Evening Regulator (page 58). Another good choice is juice containing celery, which provides a perfect balance of potassium and sodium, such as the Calming Nightcap (page 106) and Waldorf Salad Juice (page 150).

Irregularity. Most fruit juices and many vegetable juices are beneficial for regularity, flushing the kidneys, and stimulating bowel activity. I particularly like the Evening Regulator (page 58), The Cape Codder (page 53), and Morning Blush (page 74). Few juices beat Cantaloupe Juice (page 52) for great taste and happy results. Wheatgrass juice is one of the best for overall flushing of toxins and keeping the system in good working order. Try AAA Juice (page 95).

Laryngitis. Nothing beats fresh pineapple juice for relieving the symptoms of laryngitis. Combine it with other fruits or even celery for delicious drinks. Also a little ginger mixed with any juice—never drink ginger juice straight up—is good for laryngitis. Try, for instance, Satin Skin Juice (page 145) and Cholesterol-Lowering Cocktail (page 116)—as you can see from the names, most juices are multitalented!

Migraines. Fennel juice, mixed with apple (page 121) or carrot juice to make it palatable, may relieve the symptoms of migraine headaches. Celery juice may also help—try Alkaline Special (page 96) or Pineapple-Celery Juice (page 140).

Motion sickness. Motion sickness is no fun—it practically ruins the idea of travel for many people. But some travelers report no motion sickness at all if they drink a juice with ginger in it just before departure. I suggest Ginger Jolt (page 64) or Cholesterol-Lowering Cocktail (page 116).

Muscle cramping. Green Power (page 125) can help soothe cramping muscles; it can also strengthen them, which reduces the chance of cramping.

Nausea and morning sickness. Whenever I feel the slightest bit of nausea, I drink a juice with ginger in it. Before I can count to fifty, I feel much better. Many women have told me that juices with ginger helped them cope with feelings of morning sickness when they were pregnant. Ginger Jolt (page 64) is a great drink. Next time the room starts to spin a bit, try a little of this wonderful juice.

Night blindness. Drinking plenty of carrot juice or carrot-based juices will help overall eyesight. Mixing apple juice with fennel juice (page 121) is terrific for combating night blindness.

Sinus problems. To clear mucus from the sinuses and breathe more freely, try juices containing ginger or radish. See the section on sore throats for more information.

Sore throat. Both radish and ginger juice, mixed with other juices, clear the sinus cavities and strengthen mucus membranes, and by doing this, they often soothe sore throats. Try Zippy Spring Tonic (page 151) and Cholesterol-Lowering Cocktail (page 116) for examples of how to mix these strong-tasting juices with tastier ones. Another great home remedy for a sore throat is a hot drink made from the juice of a 1-inch slice of horseradish root, the juice of a whole lemon, warm water, and honey.

Sunburn. Carrot juice, by itself or mixed with other juices, helps protect against sunburn. But don't forget to use sunscreen as well.

Tendinitis. I find that any juice containing cucumber, bell pepper, or other vegetables high in silicon can help reduce painful swelling caused by tendinitis. For example, Jay's Tomato Cooler (page 131) is a good one, as is the Body Cleanser (page 100). Also try the juices designed for healthy skin and nails that contain a little bell pepper juice (silicon is great for the complexion too) such as The Skin Cleanser (page 146) or Nail Beauty Juice (page 136).

Tooth decay. Greens such as parsley and kale that are high in calcium make juices that promote dental health. So do carrots. Dandelion greens, with a good amount of magnesium, are also great. Try the Zippy Spring Tonic (page 151).

Believe it or not, a wonderfully sweet juice called The Arouser (page 50) made from grapes and cherries is a powerful anticavity drink.

Upset stomach. Although you may not feel up to it, when you feel queasy, try drinking juice made from equal amounts of fennel and apple to soothe an upset stomach. My other traditional remedies are Jicama-Carrot-Parsley Juice (page 132) or the Jicama Jig (page 133), and any juice containing a little potato juice, such as the Idaho Trailblazer (page 128).

Urinary tract infection. Women suffering from mild urinary tract infections do well drinking fresh cranberry juice. Try The Cape Codder (page 53) or Cranberry-Grape-Pineapple Juice (page 55). Pomegranate juice (Eve's Promise, page 59) may also be helpful. Clean and scrub the skin well—then you can juice the pomegranate skin and all!

Viral infections. Drinking pineapple juice is a good preventative measure to take against viruses. Try Honolulu-California Connector (page 67) or Miami Cool (page 73). Also try citrus juices and carrot-based juices: Anti-Virus Cocktail (page 48) and Jay's Secret (page 130).

Weakened immune system. Garlic is important for a strong immune system. Try Jay's Secret (page 130). Onion juice can help too. You can use onion juice in place of garlic juice in the recipes I've given—or develop your own. Wheatgrass juice helps strengthen the immune system as well. Try AAA Juice (page 95).

More Serious Ailments

Diseases such as cancer, heart disease, and diabetes are terribly serious. I do not claim that juicing "cures" these or any other diseases. But it might relieve some of their symptoms and make you feel better. Better yet, the right nutrients may retard or reverse the manifestations of some of these diseases by feeding the immune system and making the body stronger and healthier overall. And good nutrition can be very important in helping prevent serious diseases. Check with your physician before incorporating juice into your diet.

Anemia. Try juices high in iron, particularly those made with spinach, kale, and other greens, such as Popeye's Pop (page 141) and The Bunny Hop (page 104). Beet juice is also helpful for treating anemia. Try Chicago Winter Tonic (page 115) and Liver Mover (page 134). Always mix beet juice with other juices.

Arthritis. I drink pineapple juice to relieve arthritis—in fact, what I drink is a glass of grapefruit-pineapple juice called Morning Blush (page 74) nearly every morning of my life to soothe the aches and stiffness caused by old football injuries. I don't know why it helps . . . but it seems to. The relatively high incidence of sulfur and selenium in cabbage and other cruciferous vegetables make them helpful too in relieving the inflammation of arthritis. Because celery contains a good balance of sodium and potassium, it is therapeutic for many who suffer from arthritis, neuritis, and rheumatism.

Please be aware: the nightshade family of vegetables (tomatoes, potatoes, green peppers, and eggplant) can sometimes cause joint pain. If eating or juicing these causes you additional pain or discomfort, then avoid them.

Cancer. Fruits and vegetables with high concentrations of beta carotene (provitamin A) may help prevent certain types of cancer. These include apricots and cantaloupe in the fruit category (the American Cancer Society particularly cites cantaloupes as helpful for preventing intestinal cancer and melanoma); carrots, broccoli, sweet potatoes, and leafy greens as the main vegetables. Cruciferous vegetables such as cauliflower and cabbage can also be protective against many cancers. Try Cantaloupe Juice (page 52), The Bushwacker (page 105), The Broccoli Cheer (page 103), and AAA Juice (page 95). Drinking a little wheatgrass juice (combined with another juice) daily helps a lot too.

Colitis and diverticulitis. There is some evidence that cabbage juice, which contains the amino acid glutamine, may relieve the pain of colitis and diverticulitis. Try Diverticula Tonic (page 119) as well as the Anti-Ulcer Cabbage Cocktail (page 97).

Diabetes. An amazing juice made from Brussels sprouts and green beans, the Pancreas Rejuvenator (page 138), may be beneficial for diabetics. Check with your doctor before including it in your diet. Pears are sweetened in large part by levulose, a fruit sugar more easily tolerated than others by diabetics. Again, check with your doctor first before including pear juice in your diet and if it is approved, try Evening Regulator (page 58).

Gallstones. Juices containing beets in small quantities contribute to a healthy gall bladder. Try the Body Cleanser (page 100) or Chicago Winter Tonic (page 115).

Heart disease. Pure orange juice (page 56) provides a perfect balance of nutrients that protects against heart disease as, among other things, it strengthens the blood vessels and capillaries. Other citrus juices are valuable as well. Vegetable juices too are important for healthy hearts. I particularly advise you to include juices with beets in them for iron-rich corpuscles. Remember that beet juice must be mixed with other juices and even then taken only in small amounts. I also recommend drinking juices containing "green" juice such as broccoli and spinach juice. Try the Blood Regenerator (page 99), the Body Cleanser (page 100), and the Cholesterol-Lowering Cocktail (page 116).

High blood pressure and strokes. A little garlic juice, mixed with other vegetable juices, may lower blood pressure. Jay's Secret (page 130) is a good example of a juice that incorporates garlic. Citrus drinks like orange juice (page 56) help develop strong blood vessels and capillaries and protect the body against stroke. Another good measure to take for high blood pressure is to drink Watermelon Juice (page 92).

High cholesterol. Replacing high-fat foods with fat-free juices will help to lower cholesterol. I particularly like the Cholesterol-Lowering Cocktail (page 116) and juice containing a little garlic, such as Jay's Secret (page 130). Or, you may substitute onion for garlic, if you prefer.

Kidney stones. Juices containing cranberry juice help flush toxins from the body and contribute to good kidney functioning. Watermelon juice has an excellent cleansing effect. I suggest The Cape Codder (page 53) and Body Cleanser (page 100).

Osteoporosis. Vegetable juices are excellent sources of calcium, which helps retard the onset of osteoporosis. Try any of the juices noted as "calcium drinks." I particularly urge you to consume a lot of kale or broccoli in carrot-based juices. Where do cows get their calcium? From greens—of course!

Prostate problems. Cranberry juice removes purines, uric acid, and toxins from the bladder, kidneys, testicles, and prostate—which means a healthier prostate and less risk of prostate cancer. Watermelon Juice (page 92) also contributes to a healthy prostate.

Stomach ulcers. Drinking juices containing cabbage or potatoes may relieve the discomfort caused by ulcers. Try the Anti-Ulcer Cabbage Cocktail (page 97) or Idaho Trailblazer (page 128).

Health and Beauty Aids

We all want to look better. I maintain that simply by incorporating juice into your everyday diet you will feel better and be healthier—and a happy "by-product" will be that you look better too! Further, some specific juices and nutrients slow down or help certain cosmetic problems such as dry or thinning hair and red, irritated eyes, and they help promote healthy-looking, smooth skin, shiny hair, and strong nails.

Hair loss. Try juices containing cucumber, such as Jay's Tomato Cooler (page 131) and Body Cleanser (page 100). Also try Hair Growth and Hair-Loss Prevention Tonic (page 126).

Haggard-looking skin. The high concentration of silicon in vegetables such as bell peppers, broccoli, cabbage, and greens make them naturals for healthy skin. Try The Skin Cleanser (page 146). Carrots, ginger, and cucumber are good too. Try Satin Skin Juice (page 145) and Body Cleanser (page 100).

Irritated eyes. Red, irritated, tired-looking eyes can add years to your looks. As a remedy for this, try juices rich in greens and carrots, such as Eye Beautifier Juice (page 120).

Lifeless hair. The silicon in apricots and bell peppers and greens such as lettuce and parsley is terrific for shining hair. Try Red Pepper Ringer (page 142), The Skin Cleanser (page 146), and Hair Growth and Hair-Loss Prevention Tonic (page 126).

Overall aging. To slow down the outward effects of aging as well as to make you feel better from the inside out, drink a wide variety of juices including plenty of celery juice, watermelon juice, and carrot juice with parsley.

Prematurely graying hair. Worrying that your hair is turning gray too early? Make the Graying Hair Remedy (page 124) part of your daily diet.

Rough, aging skin. Any juice containing apricots is great for smooth, elastic skin. Try Apricot Ambrosia (page 49). Satin Skin Juice (page 145) is good too, and mixing a little sweet potato with carrot juice (page 149) is terrific for the skin.

Weak nails. For nice strong nails that resist chipping and cracking, try Nail Beauty Juice (page 136) and Brittle Nails Juice (page 102), and any juice containing cucumbers.

8

Juice as a Way of Life

Deciding to incorporate fresh juices into your diet is one thing; figuring out how to do it is altogether another. Luckily, it is as easy as buying some fruits and vegetables, cutting them up, running them through the juicer, and drinking the results. Do this in the morning instead of having coffee, or in the evening instead of indulging in a glass of wine. If you work at home, juice in the middle of the afternoon for a healthful pick-me-up. Soon you will find yourself juicing both in the morning and the evening, and then considering toting an icy thermos to work with you (see page 265 for information on bringing juice to the office). On weekends and holidays when you are home and able to experiment, drinking more than one or two glasses of juice will become a habit—and pleasurable. If you juice once, twice, three, or more times a day you are well on your way to a more healthful life. Once you realize the benefits of juicing, you will feel great and most likely will avoid many of the aches, pains, and other complaints from which your friends and acquaintances suffer.

I know there are many different styles of eating, but as I see it, most people fall into one of four categories wherein there are: (1) those who eat meat and poultry, (2) vegetarians who include fish and dairy products in their diet, (3) strict vegetarians, commonly known as vegans, and (4) raw foodists such as Linda and I who eat less than one fifth of our foods cooked. Obviously there are other dietary philosophies besides these four and I hope everyone embracing those will be able to adapt the information in this book to their own needs and beliefs.

Making Changes

Primary to my beliefs is the importance of consuming as much raw food as possible. Ninety percent of my food intake is raw. When I do eat cooked food it is in the form of rice, potatoes, grains, legumes, or pasta. I consume no flesh, no dairy products, no sugar, no caffeine. And I feel great.

Many readers may decide from the very start that they have little interest in a diet as extreme as mine but nevertheless want to eat more healthfully. For these people, I recommend a goal of consuming 50 percent of their food raw. This may seem like a lot at first, and it may take a while to build up to, but trust me, it will seem reasonable very quickly. If the 50 percent diet is designed to include three or four juices, most people will discover that before they know it, they are sneaking up on a diet that is 60, 70, and even 80 percent raw. Why? Because they will begin to feel so healthy, so full of energy and renewed vigor, that a glass of carrot juice will be far more appealing than an ice-cream cone or a cheeseburger.

In place of your usual fare, start eating raw vegetable salads, whole fruits, sprouts, grains such as brown rice and bulgur wheat, legumes such as beans and lentils, pasta, and cereals such as natural oatmeal and granola (unhulled oats with no added sugar).

Other foods can be enjoyed as treats, as long as you regularly consume juices and raw foods. Let's face it, today's on-the-run life-style makes eating healthfully tricky at times. How often do you find yourself grabbing something quick to eat on the way to work or as you dash out the door for an evening meeting? How often do you get together with a friend or colleague for a "drink" or "cup of coffee"? Or find yourself dealing with hunger pangs as you are delayed in an airport? While there are creative ways of maintaining a healthful diet in these situations, it is not always possible and you may choose to down a frozen yogurt, a few crackers, a hunk of cheese, or a fast-food taco. Even with these sometimes unavoidable lapses, you can return to juicing as soon as you get home and still maintain excellent health.

What is more, you may, for example, love roast duck or cheese omelets and the idea of eliminating either from your diet is unthinkable. While I truly believe you will feel better, be healthier, and after a short time, not miss these sorts of foods in the least, I believe even more strongly in the value of incorporating juice and an increased amount of raw foods into your diet in whatever way best fits your life-style and confirms your personal convictions.

No one (not even I!) can eat enough raw foods to nourish his or her body correctly. Nutritionists estimate that we would have to consume approximately fifteen pounds of raw plants every day to supply the body with what it needs. The good news is we can juice.

Nutrient-rich juice supplies our cells with everything they need to stay healthy and functioning. It cleanses our systems and promotes regularity. It strengthens bones, makes our hair shine, and contributes to a healthy heart. Just one or two glasses every day helps a lot. More than that? Even better!

Juicing Every Day

I am not trying to sell a fad diet. I am not going to tell you precisely what to eat and when to eat it. I offer no specific menus and very few rules. What I am "selling" is a sensible, delicious, and nutritious route to a more energetic, healthier, and happier life.

With this in mind, work toward a diet that includes six glasses of juice a day, making sure at least one is carrot, or a carrot-based, juice. Sweet, delicious carrot juice mixes magically with a wide array of fruits and other vegetables, but more important, it provides your body with a valuable spectrum of vital nutrients including all-important beta carotene. Four of the six daily juices should be vegetable juices (made easy with carrot juice!) and two fruit juices, a 2:1 ratio. And remember, with very few exceptions, juices of vegetables and fruits should not be combined. Both have their own roles and combining the natural oils in vegetables with the acidity of fruits is akin to mixing oil and water. It may cause you to experience bloating, gastric distress, and nausea. The shining exceptions, as you undoubtedly know by now, are carrot juice and apple juice.

I drink at least two quarts (eight cups) of fresh juice a day, which is more than I recommend to anyone just beginning to juice. Start slowly with two or three glasses (8 ounces each) and work up to six or more. Try to keep the 2:1 ratio in mind. Perhaps you could begin with a glass of frothy orange or pineapple juice in the morning, drink a glass of carrot-apple or carrot-celery juice at lunchtime, and then another vegetable juice with dinner. If, after a few days or a week, you add a vegetable juice midmorning and also midafternoon or early evening, and a soothing fruit juice before bed, you have done it! That's six glasses during the day. Painless, isn't it? Delicious, too.

What to Eat

In addition to juice, consider beginning the day with natural cereal, oatmeal, or unsweetened granola and some fresh fruit. Snack on a few pieces of dried fruit or nuts during the morning and then for lunch eat a generous bowl of raw salad with a light yogurt, tahini, or vinaigrette dressing. Another good choice for lunch is a brown rice and vegetable pilaf, or pasta with lightly cooked fresh vegetables or tomato sauce made from garden tomatoes. Snack on fruit or handfuls of sprouts, and by evening, after a glass of carrot or other vegetable juice, eat a smaller portion of rice or pasta, some mildly spiced beans, or vegetable soup.

During the week, also eat nuts and seeds for great flavor and crunch, as well as for needed oils. Other oils, such as walnut and olive oil, are valuable in small amounts. Finally, incorporate easily digestible, protein-rich tofu into your diet. It is very important to get enough protein. If you want to include fish, eat the very freshest you can find and steam, bake, or broil it to avoid adding extra fats.

I suggest consuming most of your daily food intake in the morning and afternoon and eating very little in the evening. If possible, eat small meals three, four, or five times a day. I nibble constantly, and always on one kind of food. Rarely in the past forty-five years have I sat down to a meal with five or six food combinations. I prefer to avoid the enzymatic clash that occurs in the digestive system when it deals with a lot of different foods. I suppose you could say I eat like an animal: one food at a time.

As I explained before, begin the day with fruit juice and end it with a soothing evening tonic of apple-pear or carrot-apple juice. If you are hungry in the evening before bed or while watching television, eat some fruit—fruit is easy and quick to digest. Please don't reach for a bag of chips or a bowl of ice cream. One of the biggest mistakes we make is to eat a lot of heavy food late in the day. As you sleep, your entire system should have uninterrupted, restful time to rejuvenate, detoxify, purify, and regenerate. But if most of your energy is monopolized by your digestive system working time and a half because you over-ate in the evening, you might wake up feeling strangely unrested. And guess what? Your body is telling you something.

Juicing and Cooked Food

I hope by now you realize I am not insisting that everyone give up cooked food. I hope you will cook far less than you used to, and perhaps as the months and years go by, you will find yourself relying very little on the stove and oven. But for many people, cooking is an integral and pleasurable part of life.

If you eat cooked foods, please remember one thing: Drink vegetable juice with the meal. And I do not mean V8. I mean freshly made carrot-celery juice or any juice with a combination of vegetables (see the recipes beginning on page 94). As you eat, chew the food well, then sip the juice after nearly every forkful of food—swirling it in your mouth until it feels warm and tastes sweet—to activate the digestive enzymes in the saliva. The live food in the juice provides the body with extra enzymes to aid digestion and absorption.

When you cook, cook food only until warm if possible. By preventing the food from getting too hot, you will not kill all the helpful enzymes. Naturally, this is not sensible with everything. Meat and poultry must be thoroughly cooked; raw fish may carry harmful parasites; raw or undercooked eggs may be tainted with salmonella; a half-baked potato is unpleasant to eat; and no one likes crunchy pasta or rice. But most vegetables need only a short stint over the heat; grains such as bulgur soften during soaking and do not always require lengthy cooking.

When you eat a baked potato or a bowl of steaming soup, scatter a good measure of chopped raw onions over it. The onions add good flavor as well as a portion of raw food.

Foods to Avoid

I openly admit that I would prefer to call this section "foods to eliminate," but being realistic and respectful of your very personal likes and prejudices, I suggest only that you cut back on the following foods.

All of us are raised on certain foods that may play an important role in family traditions or that we find particularly comforting. Do I forgo the turkey with all the trimmings at

Thanksgiving? You bet I do, but that does not mean I expect everyone to. Do I crave hot chocolate after a day on the ski slopes? Not at all; I warm up with a cup of hot herbal tea, but you may look forward to the sweet, chocolaty drink all the way down the mountain. What I hope is that you will consume these things in moderation.

Here is a list of foods I recommend eating sparingly, if at all. At first glance, the list may seem to include every culinary pleasure on the planet and may overwhelm you with feelings of deprivation. This is not the case. These are foods that I shun for sound dietary reasons, and if you reduce your intake of them and supplement your diet with delicious fresh juices, crisp salads, naturally sweet fruits, and wholesome grains, I promise you will feel, look, and be healthier. Again, I am not insisting that these foods be banished from your kitchen and life—just that you think about what you put in your mouth, how often, and why.

Alcohol. Alcohol is high in calories and sugars. Its food value is nominal, while the harm it wreaks on the body and spirit is phenomenal. As well as contributing to liver and heart disease, high blood pressure and high cholesterol, alcohol is dangerously addictive. Breaking the addiction is difficult and far too often comes about only after much heartbreak and physical damage. I strongly urge everyone to refrain from consuming alcohol, and if you can't or don't, then consume it in extreme moderation. After a stressful day, try carrot-apple juice or carrot-celery juice. The juice will help you relax and restore energy too.

All processed foods. In the name of progress, we have altered, denatured, and devitalized our food with additives and chemicals. This means that we must eat more to satisfy the body's nutritional needs. Much of the processing technology is aimed at extending the shelf life of the food, making it practically indestructible. This is great—if you are starving in a drought-ridden country with no other available nutrition. Fortunately, in America and most of the Western world this is not the case. We are blessed with an abundant and varied supply of fresh produce from which we can extract the optimal amount of vitamins and minerals to ensure good health and well-being. Why do otherwise?

Brown sugar and honey. Brown sugar is no better than white sugar. Both provide empty calories with very little food value. Like sugar, honey is a sweetening agent that is largely unnecessary when your diet is rich in naturally sweet fruits. However, if you like to sweeten herbal tea, use honey. I prefer to use tupelo honey. Sometimes I also use maple syrup as a sweetener.

Caffeine. Coffee and tea, both full of caffeine, are not good for anyone. The exception is soothing, caffeine-free herbal tea. Caffeine is also present in colas, over-the-counter pain relievers (read the labels), and, in small amounts, chocolate. The tannic acid in caffeine contributes to constipation. On the other hand, it acts as a diuretic, flushing valuable nutrients from the body before they are properly absorbed and robbing the body of necessary fluids. Caffeine is addictive and can cause headache, nausea, insomnia, crankiness, and the jitters. These same symptoms may occur during withdrawal from caffeine but in a few days will pass. Caffeine is linked to premenstrual syndrome and high cholesterol and certainly aggravates the symptoms of stomach ulcers by stimulating the release of acids in the body. I begin each day with fruit juice, a quick and healthful energizer. Try it, you'll like it.

Chocolate. If you could stomach pure, unsweetened chocolate, called chocolate liquor in the trade, eating chocolate would not be too bad. However, chocolate liquor is not what we refer to when we speak of the confection. Chocolate as we know it is chocolate liquor that has been sweetened with sugar and emulsified with cocoa butter or vegetable shortening (both fats). Some chocolate contains added milk solids, which make it milk chocolate. There is little nutritional value in chocolate—just sugar and fat and a small amount of caffeine.

Cooked vegetables and fruits. When you cook vegetables and fruits you destroy many of the live cells in these nourishing plants. When you eat the cooked food you are getting only a fraction of the vitamins and minerals you would get if you ate them raw. Nutrients leach out into the cooking water or evaporate with the moisture naturally occurring in the food. Of course cooked foods will not harm you, but they do not have nearly as much nutritional value as do raw fruits and vegetables.

Dairy products. All mammals rely on their mother's milk for early nourishment, and humans are no different. As we mature, we are the only mammal that continues to drink milk and eat cheese and yogurt. Personally, I do not recommend dairy products for weaned children and I do not find them necessary for adults. The mucus associated with dairy products slows or inhibits digestion. The high percentage of animal fat in most dairy products contributes to a number of diseases, including heart disease and some cancers. If you must consume dairy products, make sure they are nonfat or low-fat, and drink only skim milk. Goat's milk has a smaller molecular structure and is easier to digest than cow's milk. Soy milk and almond milk are both good substitutes for either cow's or goat's milk and are available at health food stores. (We prefer almond milk.) Use them in recipes or to pour over hot cereal; your family will soon request them.

Eggs. For decades the American medical community has warned victims of high cholesterol and heart disease about the danger of eating eggs. The yolks are high in fat, and while whole eggs supply the body with protein, it is a simple matter to get protein elsewhere. What is more, in recent years there has been a lot written in the popular press about salmonella in eggs, bacteria that cause the body to experience a host of symptoms ranging from flulike aches and pains to chronic discomfort. Eggs and every preparation containing eggs must be cooked to a temperature of 160°F or above to ensure safety.

Fried foods. By their very nature fried foods are laced with fat. It is impossible to fry anything without relying on a fatty agent—oil, butter, or lard—to heat to the extreme temperature necessary to seal the food and produce the crisp coating that makes fried food appealing to so many people. Unfortunately, during cooking the food not only absorbs some of the fat, it also swims in it so that the coating may be greasy and oily. If you really enjoy fried food, try broiling or grilling it instead with no or just a little fat. If you insist on eating fried foods, make absolutely sure the cooking fat is hot enough to seal the food quickly. This will prevent too much fat from entering the food. Soy oil and corn oil are the best oils to use for frying. And be sure never to save or reuse oil that has been heated. The best advice is to avoid fried foods wherever possible.

Meat. When we eat meat, we are putting "secondhand" nutrients into our bodies. By this I mean we are getting vitamins and minerals from the plants the animal consumed during its life. These nutrients helped the animal develop fine muscles and tissues. They can help us do the same, but why wait for them to be processed through another animal's flesh—flesh that often is shot full of hormones and antibiotics? We can receive the nutrients directly and efficiently by eating raw plants, either in the form of juice or otherwise. What is more, consumption of red meat is linked to heart disease, high cholesterol, and cancers such as colon and prostate. Both the established medical community and the federal government agree that Americans should reduce their intake of red meat. I extend this recommendation to poultry, which often is tainted with salmonella bacteria as well as antibiotics and hormones.

Salt. Salt is a naturally existing mineral. Because it exists in such abundance on the earth, it is present as organic sodium chloride in many vegetables. These traces are all you need for your health. There is no reason to add table salt to your food if you eat a balanced vegetarian diet. In fact, salt may contribute to high blood pressure and heart disease. It can cause the body to retain fluids and feel bloated. We lose salt when we exercise, but if you drink a juice with celery in it after a strenuous workout, you will easily replace the sodium the body needs.

Water. I am not exaggerating when I say I have not had a glass of tap water in nearly fifty years. What I mean is I don't turn on the faucet and fill a glass with water for drinking. Instead, I get almost all the water I need from juice and raw fruits and vegetables: pure, unadulterated, natural water filtered through the live cells of living plants. When I drink water, I drink bottled distilled or mineral water. I suggest you do the same, or buy a good-quality filter for your sink.

In my opinion, much of the water in the public water systems is not fit for human consumption. It is overtreated with chemicals that can endanger your health. What is more, a percentage of lead may leach out into household water from old pipes and solderings, which is a potentially dangerous situation. Use tap water only for bathing and washing dishes and clothes. For cooking and brewing herbal tea, I suggest steam distilled water. If you are concerned about the lack of minerals in distilled water, rest easy. Juicing provides ample minerals.

White sugar and flour. White sugar is refined sugarcane, broken down until any trace of the original plant is gone and what is left is a sweet substance with little food value. A teaspoon of white sugar contains about sixteen calories and nothing else. We add it to all sorts of fat-laden creations to make them ultimately palatable. White flour is similar to white sugar in that during refining all of the germ and bran of the wheat has been removed so that only a white powder remains. White flour may yield a tender biscuit, but I suggest using whole wheat flour for baking. At least this flour has a modicum of nutrition.

You will find that after several days or weeks without a lot of sugar, salt, caffeine, and meat, you will feel better, look better, and probably will lose most of your desire for them. Your system will be cleansed and will crave fresh, wholesome foods; your palate will have developed a taste for sweet, pure juice. You will eye the produce section of the market with new interest, mentally concocting juice ideas as you stroll along the aisles. This is what being on a healthful, natural diet is all about: renewed vigor and a sense of culinary adventure that heightens as you come to realize the benefits of feeling and looking great.

The Importance of Exercise

The fact is, my friends, no matter how many glasses of carrot juice you drink in a day, if you don't get up and move about, your body will deteriorate despite your efforts to eat healthfully. When asked the secret of long life, George Burns once said it was getting out of bed every morning. I agree. Get up, get out, get moving.

If you are able, take a brisk walk, ride your bicycle, go swimming. Even if you do not swim, hang on to the side of the pool and kick your legs, or jog in waist-deep water. Try to exercise for at least twenty minutes every day. Your heart needs the stimulation. If you're physically able, build up to more.

I am an insatiable racquetball player, and even when on the road, I try to find a health club where I can pick up a game or two. When I am home, I spend a good twenty minutes or longer at high speeds on a huge treadmill I have installed in the house. I also use my rowing machine daily. You do not have to do as much as I do—any form of exercise tones the body, and more important, gets the heart pumping.

A Word on Fasting

Every so often I fast. It is usually once a week and I never give up juice completely for that twenty-four-hour period. I drink Waldorf Salad Juice (page 150) to maintain the sodium-potassium balance the body needs. During these fasts I dilute the juice by half with distilled water so that it is easier on the system.

Why do I fast? I believe it cleanses my body and refreshes my soul. Fasting, with its long and sometimes tumultuous history, is currently in some disrepute with the established medical community. Nonetheless, many people fast. Certainly a day without solid food does no harm—if you are healthy to begin with. (Obviously diabetics and anyone suffering from ill health should not fast. Everyone should consult his or her doctor before fasting.)

My body works hard twenty-four hours a day, six days a week; I view fasting as its "day off." During this day, the body cleanses, purifies, and essentially resurrects itself. During the fast, the system flushes out the liver, kidneys, and bladder and eliminates toxins. The purging is ultimately restful and relaxing. After a day of fasting and a good night's sleep, I wake up full of vigor, eager to start the next week fully charged and ready to meet new challenges.

9

Juicing for Weight Loss

When you integrate juice into your regular daily diet and life-style, I promise you will feel better, look better—and unwanted pounds will melt away. Why? The answer is simple. Fruit and vegetable juices are essentially fat-free, have very few calories, and while supplying you with all the nutrients your body needs, also satisfy hunger pangs and cravings for sweets. An 8-ounce glass of fruit juice contains about a hundred calories; a glass of vegetable juice about half that amount.

How to Lose Weight While Juicing

The only effective way to lose weight is to eat less food than you have been, and to change the type of food you are eating. In other words, alter your eating behavior. With a juicer in the kitchen and fresh produce in the refrigerator, doing this is a breeze. As with any weight reduction diet, check with your doctor before beginning a regimen that includes a lot of juices.

Drink a glass of foamy fruit juice to start the day and then eat a good, wholesome breakfast. Drink a glass of juice mid-morning and midafternoon to quell any hunger pangs. Then drink vegetable juices with lunch and dinner, and finally drink a soothing glass of juice in the evening before bed. Does the routine sound familiar? It should, as it incorporates the six glasses of juice I recommend throughout this book for optimum healthful benefits. These six glasses provide you with enough nutrients to see you through the day if accompanied by light, low-fat meals high in fiber.

Eat raw lettuce and other vegetable salads, grains, and legumes. These provide bulk without a lot of calories and fat. After a short while, you will eat less at meals and, because you will feel better, will prefer healthful foods to junk foods. Best of all, once you reach your desired weight, the juices will help your system maintain its perfect balance of nutrients so that you will not be tempted to overindulge in fat-laden foods and consequently avoid the cycle that happens with nearly every "diet" in the world: The pounds you worked so hard to shed creep back on.

Do Not Forget to Exercise

Using juices to help curb the appetite and ultimately let you lose weight is effective only if you include some exercise in your life. This is particularly important for anyone leading a sedentary life. In Chapter 8, I discuss how vital exercise is for a healthy heart and cardiovascular system. It is also a valuable and pleasurable tool for weight loss.

You have heard it before, and I am not going to tell you any differently. The only way to lose weight and keep it off is to change your eating habits and exercise regularly. Commit to a good twenty-minute walk every day; join an aerobics class; find a partner for regular squash or racquetball games; join the "Y" and swim three or four times a week; dust off your bicycle and take it out on the road or invest in a stationary bike. There are numerous ways to fit exercise into your particular life-style. But the fact remains that you are the only one who can make the decision and then stay with an exercise routine. Happily, once you begin exercising, your energy level will increase and you will begin to enjoy the exercise more than ever.

What's Wrong with the American Diet

To understand why so many of us struggle with extra pounds and an inability to keep them off, I think we should examine the general diet of most Americans. It is pretty dismal, rife with foods high in saturated fats, sodium, and empty calories.

Undoubtedly you are aware that the four basic food groups are not really all they are cracked up to be. Since elementary school, we have been taught to respect them and to eat a "balanced" diet by consuming foods from each group: (1) meat, poultry, and fish; (2) dairy products and eggs; (3) fruits and vegetables; and (4) grains, legumes, seeds, and nuts. Eating foods from these categories in more or less equal amounts constitutes the standard American diet, or SAD. And sad it is. Most people concentrate on meats and dairy products and ignore—or give a cursory nod to—fruits, vegetables, grains, and legumes.

The good news is that people are revising their thinking about the four food groups and are learning about what is called "the New Four Food Groups." Americans are encouraged to eat more fruits, vegetables, grains, and legumes. If used as a foundation, the New Four Food Groups can supply ample nutrients, fiber, essential fatty acids, and protein—the components of a healthy diet.

The Logic of Juicing

If the New Four Food Groups illustrates that we should include a generous amount of grains, legumes, vegetables, and fruits in our diets, it makes sense that juicing as many of these foods as possible ensures that we reap the full benefit of their nutrients. Once you decide that this makes sense, you will instinctively feed your body with a healthful, low-fat diet. The raw salads, beans, rice, and pasta you eat to supplement the juices and supply the body with needed fiber, protein, and complex carbohydrates are deliciously filling without being fattening.

Pasta, rice, and baked potatoes are not the culprits when it comes to weight gain. It's the sauce, butter, and sour cream that do the damage. Toss pasta and rice with slightly cooked vegetables, fresh tomato sauce, or vinegar, garlic, a little olive oil, and fresh herbs. Put a dollop of nonfat or low-fat yogurt, a squeeze of lemon juice, chopped herbs, or lightly grilled tomato slices on the baked potato.

Plan meals around the juice, beginning, as I always do, with the juice as the focus. Soon you will be drinking pleasantly filling juices supplemented by a diet rich in fiber and carbohydrates—and nearly all your desire for fattening and sweet foods will disappear.

10

The Juiceman Answers Your Questions

Many of the questions addressed here are discussed elsewhere in the book. But, because these are the most frequently asked, I offer them again in a straightforward, question-and-answer format. Others are stray issues not previously covered that nonetheless deserve attention.

Q: Why is juicing so important? Why can't I just eat the food?

A: Juicing is the most helpful thing you can do for your body nutritionally. When you eat, the body takes approximately one and a half days to process the food completely from the time of ingestion to elimination. And even when working to perfection, the body extracts a small percentage of the valuable juice from the fiber. A large percentage is locked in the fiber that is expelled from the body. When you juice, highly concentrated nutrients enter your bloodstream very quickly because your body doesn't need to extract the juice from the fiber.

Q: Why can't I use a blender or food processor to make juice? Why do I need a juicer?

A: A blender and food processor do not extract the juice from the fiber. They purée or mash the fiber with the juice, simply liquefying the fruit or vegetable. A juicer separates the life-giving juice from the fiber.

Q: Can't I buy bottled juices at the market? Aren't they just as good for me?

A: The fresher the juice the greater its nutritional value. Fruits and vegetables processed for commercial canning are pasteurized (heated) to extend their shelf life and meet government standards. This processing causes some nutrient loss. Freshly made juices are pure and full of the concentrated nutrients which I believe are so important to good health and well-being. Plus, with juice you make you have absolute control of what is in the juice.

Q: When you juice fruits and vegetables, you throw away the fiber. Isn't fiber important too?

A: Fiber is more than important, it is essential. Worldwide epidemiological studies indicate that fiber is a key component in preventing colon cancer. This is why I always say to "eat around the juicer" for fiber. Eat plenty of raw foods that are high in fiber, such as whole fruits and vegetables. Also be sure to include a variety of legumes and whole grains.

Q: Can't I get all the nutrients I need from vitamin pills?

A: Nutrients found in fresh fruits and vegetables are far more potent than those found in pills. Because nutrients influence each other by working synergistically, they help each other to create working reactions within the body. When combined naturally in food, they are far more effective and better absorbed than when singled out in pill form.

And there's another reason. Nutrients are constantly being discovered and named. For example, you've heard of beta carotene, but does alpha carotene mean much to you? This nutrient, found primarily in fruits and vegetables, has recently shown protective effects against vulvar cancer. Phenols, indoles, aromatic isothiocyanates, terpenes, and organosulfur compounds are part of a new category called "anutrients," which may show protective effects against some cancers. You guessed it: They are found in fruits, vegetables, grains, and other plants.

The point is, these nutrients are only just being shown to have value, being given names or categories, and certainly won't appear in supplement pills for a while. Remember, juices provide not only nutrients with well-known functions, but also nutrients with roles that are not yet understood or recognized. Fresh fruits and vegetables are good for us in ways we do not even know about yet!

Finally, if you do need to take a particular supplement, be sure to swallow it with the juices that are highest in that nutrient for better absorption.

Q: How do you get enough protein if you eat a vegetarian diet?

A: Incorporating fresh fruit and vegetable juices into your diet does not mean you have to become a vegetarian. But if you do reduce your intake of meat and dairy products, you can still incorporate protein in your diet. The combination of beans and rice is a classic example of a complete protein vegetarian meal.

Plant life contains protein. Large amounts of plant foods are difficult to consume because of the indigestible cellulose fiber. But this roadblock is eliminated when we juice the plant. For example, it takes about a pound of carrots to make about eight ounces of juice and in that pound are about three grams of protein, plus vitamins A and C.

Q: Are there ways to use fresh fruit and vegetable juices in cooking?

A: There are lots of delicious uses for juices in cooking. Add fresh carrot or a combination of carrot and another vegetable juice to stocks, sauces, and soups. Make fresh tomato juice and use it as the base for fresh tomato sauce for pasta. Try poaching pears in a mixture of water and pear juice (you might want to add a little sweetener too), or using a splash of fresh apple juice in apple pie or applesauce. Juiced oranges, limes, and lemons are great in cakes and custard-based pies calling for citrus. Fruit juices can be the bases for delicious sherbets and sorbets. Let your imagination and common sense guide you and soon you will be incorporating fresh, wholesome juices into numerous dishes.

Q: Can I use the fruit and vegetable fiber that accumulates during juicing in cooking?

A: Of course! Carrots are the most successful. The fibers are finely grated carrots, the crucial ingredient in carrot cake.

The fibers are dry, however, and so you may have to adjust the liquid in the recipe. And speaking of the liquid, try some of the juice in place of the water or milk called for. People have also told me they add the carrot fiber to meat loaf or bean loaf for good flavor and texture.

Another use of the juicer is to prepare freshly grated coconut. Buy a whole coconut and, if possible, crack it open at the store to make sure it does not have any fungal growth in it, which is a common occurrence. At home, remove all the hard, brown exterior and press the white interior through the juicer. One whole coconut should yield about 2 cups of unsweetened, grated coconut and about ⅓ cup of coconut milk.

Q: What else can I do with the leftover fiber?

A: The most obvious thing to do with the fiber is to compost it. Keeping a compost pile in the backyard is easy and reduces your output of disposable garbage. Mix the fiber from the juicer as well as other biodegradable food scraps (meat and dairy are *not* recommended) with grass cuttings and leaves to make rich, fertile composted soil to use on lawns and vegetable and flower gardens.

Q: Can I put fruits and vegetables with seeds and pits through the juicer?

A: Most small seeds are fine—the juicer will simply expel them with the fiber. Peach, apricot, nectarine, and cherry pits should be removed, as should any large, obviously hard stones or seeds.

Q: Are there any fruits and vegetables I should peel before juicing?

A: It is important always to remove the outer colored rinds of oranges, grapefruits, and tangerines when juicing. These particular citrus rinds contain indigestible, volatile oils that taste bitter and may interfere with your absorption of the nutrients in the fresh juice. Also peel mangoes and papayas. There is no need to peel lemons and limes.

Remember to cut the outer rind off pineapples and melons if they are not organically grown. The same is true for the stems of inorganically grown grapes, and about one inch of the root ends of carrots and other root vegetables. These are the areas of the plant where pesticides and other chemicals tend to be most concentrated. For more information, read carefully Chapter 5, which has information on juicing the fruits and vegetables mentioned in the recipes.

Q: Is there a greater concentration of pesticides in juice than in a single fruit or vegetable?

A: Not necessarily. Most pesticides, herbicides, and fungicides are on the surface of the fruit or vegetable and so can be washed off with a biodegradable natural cleanser designed to remove them. These cleansers are available at health food stores and through a number of mail-order catalogues catering to environmentally sound products. It is because of these chemicals that I urge you to buy organically grown produce whenever possible.

Q: I am pregnant and want to know if I can incorporate juices into my diet both now and after the baby is born when I am nursing.

A: Absolutely. Now is the time to pay close attention to nutrition for you and the baby. Fresh, delicious, wholesome juices are terrific sources of vitamins and minerals—without unnecessary fats and sugars—and they taste wonderful. I do *not* recommend juices as an alternative for prenatal vitamin supplements. Your body needs a wide range of nutrients at this crucial time and the supplements are designed to meet your very special needs. But try drinking fresh juices in place of the coffee, tea, and alcohol you have given up during these nine months. Make a big glass of carrot-apple-parsley (page 129) or orange juice in the late afternoon when you feel in need of a pick-me-up. Continue this practice during nursing to supply your body and your baby with valuable nutrients. Always consult your doctor before changing your diet in any way.

Q: What are your favorite juices?

A: I like so many different juices, it is hard to name just a few. Also, I drink specific juices for targeted health reasons. But I do have some all-time favorites I call the "magic dozen." You will find these in the recipe section of this book with the following names: The Champ (carrot-apple juice); Cantaloupe Juice; Watermelon Juice; San Francisco Fog Cutter (apple-strawberry juice); Bromelain Plus (pineapple juice); either Dawn Patrol or The Eye-Opener (orange or grapefruit juice); Waldorf Salad Juice (apple-celery juice); Digestive Special (spinach-carrot juice); The Carrot Top (carrot-beet juice); Pick-Me-Up Energy Cocktail (carrot-parsley juice); Evening Regulator (apple-pear juice); and Green Power (spinach-parsley-celery-carrot juice).

Q: What juices do you recommend during hot weather?

A: All juices provide the body with water and therefore keep it cool. I suggest any juice with cucumbers and watermelon—both are natural coolants as people living in hot regions such as India and the Middle East have long realized. Juices containing celery are good as the celery juice replaces sodium lost through perspiration. I also love Jay's World Famous Lemonade (page 68) too. Try it over crushed ice.

Q: When I am really thirsty, I like drinks with fizz. How can I satisfy this craving with fruit juice?

A: It's as easy as adding a ½ cup or so of sparkling mineral water to the juice right after it comes from the juicer. Chill the mineral water first and use chilled fruits or vegetables.

Q: What juices do you suggest serving at parties?

A: Any of the fruit juices are great choices. Your friends will appreciate the flavor and novelty of fresh apple juice, pine-apple juice, and cantaloupe juice. The Champ is always a big hit too. To make the juices more festive, serve them over crushed ice, add a twist or slice of lemon or lime, or add some sparkling mineral water.

Sorbets made from fresh juice are also always popular.

Q: What are the best juices to drink with meals?

A: Vegetable juices make good accompaniments for meals. Sip the juice between every bite of food and be sure to "chew" the juice. This means swirling it around in your mouth until it tastes sweet and feels warm so that the digestive enzymes in the saliva are activated.

Q: When I am juicing, should I use an apple to clean the juicer when I want to switch from fruits to vegetables, or vice versa?

A: Yes, that's a good idea. Use apples as neutralizers since they are compatible with every fruit and vegetable. The apple washes out any residue of the previous juice. Remember to place a clean cup under the juicer's spout for the next juice. After a lot of juicing, or when you are through juicing for the time being, clean the juicer with clear, running water.

Q: How long can I store fresh juice?

A: If possible, I do not recommend storing it at all. For the most benefit, drink juice soon after making it, as it begins to deteriorate rapidly. The act of slicing an orange causes it to lose some vitamin C, for instance, and apples begin to oxidate (turn brown) right after they are cut. If you must store juice, keep it in an air-tight container in the refrigerator for no more than twenty-four hours. (Melon juice and cabbage juice do not keep well.)

Q: Is juice still good after it turns brown?

A: No, it has oxidized and lost its food value. After about twenty-four hours of storage, it may become toxic. This is why the government requires commercial canneries to pasteurize juices so that their shelf life is extended. Freshly made juices are the absolute opposite of day-old juices; they are much better for you.

Q: I want to drink juices at the office. How do I take fresh juices to work and keep them viable?

A: Luckily there is a way to do just that. Rinse out a sturdy thermos with water and then put it in the freezer the night before so that the inside liner gets nice and frosty (like a frosted beer mug). Just before leaving the house, pour freshly made juice into the thermos right up to the lip—it's important not to leave an air pocket. Screw the top on the thermos holding it over the sink since the full jug will probably overflow a little. If you leave any air in, it will warm up and the juice will lose some of its potency. If possible, store the thermos in the refrigerator at the office. Drink the juice all at once or share it with a co-worker. Do not drink a little and recap it. You might consider buying two small thermoses so you can enjoy wholesome juice in the morning and afternoon.

Q: You started juicing when you were young. I am over fifty and have not eaten a very healthful diet. Will I benefit at all if I start now?

A: It is never too late. And if you enjoy the good life—socializing, prime rib dinners, cocktails—you need the juices more than ever. Drink them to flush the toxins from your body and then go party. But even more important, initiating a more healthful diet at any age is good for your heart, your circulation, your weight, and your overall feeling of well-being.

Q: Will juice lower my cholesterol?

A: Just as incorporating juices into your diet will help you lose weight naturally, it will also help lower your cholesterol. Fresh fruit and vegetable juices contain no saturated fats or added sodium. They are full of vitamins and minerals and help everyone stick to a healthful, low-fat diet. If your doctor has advised you to lower your cholesterol by changing your diet, talk to him or her about the value of fresh juices.

Q: If I am out for the day and want to buy some carrot juice, is that all right?

A: It is not only all right, I encourage it. During a long afternoon of shopping, attending meetings, or rambling through the park, a frothy glass of carrot juice is much more valuable (and delicious, I think) than a can of soda or a cup of coffee. Find a health food store or café that juices its own or buys it daily. The next best thing to freshly made juices are those made early in the morning and delivered the same day. A reputable store will refrigerate the juice. Even then, it may be six, eight, or ten hours old and will not give you the same lift as the fresh juice you make at home.

Q: I like to pour milk on my hot and cold cereal. What do you use to moisten cereal?

A: I use fresh apple juice. I add it to dry cold cereal, and when the weather is cold, I heat it gently and pour it over hot oatmeal. Delicious! I never let it get hotter than about 100°F, which is a little warmer than lukewarm, so that I don't kill the enzymes. You can also try almond milk or fresh soy milk.

Q: Do you have any suggestions for healthful ways to eat out in restaurants?

A: This is tricky but it can be done. First, I avoid "fancy" restaurants where the chef may use heavy cream sauces and serve a lot of meat and poultry. I usually order a salad, such as spinach salad without the eggs and bacon. I either bring my own organic apple cider vinegar to dress the salad or request the oil and vinegar in cruets and make my own dressing. Fresh lemon juice is a good choice too. Plain rice is usually readily available in restaurants. And many restaurants will serve you a plate of steamed vegetables with a plain baked potato on the side. If you eat fish, ask for broiled fish without sauce. Eat the bread without butter. Avoid dessert and drink seltzer or mineral water with a twist of lemon or lime. A lot of problems can be eliminated by seeking out and patronizing health bars, vegetarian restaurants, and with limited application, salad bars.

Q: How do you care for your teeth and gums?

A: Chewing a lot of fiber exercises the gums and, of course, I make sure to get enough vitamins and minerals by juicing. I brush my teeth and gums daily with a natural toothpaste and also follow a special cleansing routine two or three times a week. I put a little baking soda in a dish and add a few drops of hydrogen peroxide to make a paste. I rub this on my teeth and gums with a soft toothbrush, making sure to get it on all the surfaces of the teeth, including between them, and just above them on the gums. I then concentrate on rubbing the paste on the gums. The entire procedure takes about four or five minutes—but those minutes are mighty valuable. Do this at least twice but never more than three times a week. If you fast, as I do about once a week, follow this procedure during the fast to prevent buildup of lactic acid formation that too often results in dental caries.

Q: Should I encourage my children to juice?

A: I should say so! Growing children need a full complement of vitamins and minerals for healthy development, and how better to help get them than through juice? Instilling a liking for fresh juices and other raw foods will help them develop lifelong healthful eating habits too. My two young sons actually prefer fresh fruit juices to most other drinks. But remember that children's dietary needs are different from adults' and do not expect—or require—your children to drink as many juices as you do.

After they are 6 months, you may be able to start giving your children very simple juices, like orange juice, always mixed with at least 50 percent purified or distilled water. As every child develops differently, check first with a pediatrician before introducing any changes into a child's diet. And watch carefully for any sign of an allergic reaction. If food allergies do develop, they will be much easier to pinpoint if you are not mixing different fruits in one juice.

When your child is between 8 and 12 months, you can gradually use less water in the juices until your child is accustomed to pure juice. Keep to simple juices like carrot, apple, orange, or cantaloupe, and let your child develop his or her own preferences.

Talk again with a pediatrician before incorporating more than one or two glasses of juice a day into your children's diet on a regular basis.

Q: How can I get my children to drink "green" juices? They practically *turn* green at the suggestion of broccoli or spinach juice.

A: Because no one should ever drink green juices without first mixing them with other juices such as carrot and apple, including these juices in your children's diets should not be too difficult. Emphasize the carrot or apple juice and play down the fact that the green juice is part of the package.

You may want to start gradually moving from pure carrot-apple juice to apple-carrot-parsley juice by adding a little bit more parsley to each successive batch of juice over the course of several weeks. If your kids find the color too strange, simply switch to using a dark-colored glass tumbler to serve the juice. Before they know it, they will be drinking juice that has a full 25 percent portion of glorious, life-giving green juice. The sweeter the apple, the more kids love it. Try using Golden Delicious apples in this juice.

You can also take a more direct approach. Most kids love to be involved with juicing. (Always supervise carefully children's use of any household appliance, including a juicer.) If you let them help you, their curiosity will get the better of them and they will be eager to try every juice.

Q: Plain fruit juices are delicious and usually satisfy my desire for any other drink, but sometimes I crave a thick, frosty shake. How can I make one with fresh fruit juice?

A: Very easily. Fresh juices mixed with nonfat dry milk and ice cubes can be whipped to a frothy foam in a blender for thick, icy drinks that rival any available at the local ice-cream shop. Two of my favorites are Creamsicle in a Glass (page 270) and Strawberry Shake (page 271). Try these and then experiment with other fruit juices using the same method—how about a kiwi or pineapple shake? Or a peach Creamsicle?

The Juiceman's Power of Juicing

Creamsicle in a Glass

One serving about 12 ounces

1 cup fresh orange juice

½ cup fresh apple juice

1 teaspoon honey

¼ teaspoon vanilla extract

2 tablespoons nonfat dry milk

2 ice cubes

Combine all the ingredients in a blender and process on high until the ice liquefies. Serve immediately.

Strawberry Shake

One serving about 12 ounces

½ cup sliced strawberries

¾ cup fresh apple and orange juice, combined

¼ cup nonfat dry milk

4 ice cubes

Put the sliced strawberries in a blender and purée until smooth. Add the remaining ingredients and process on high until thick and frothy. Pour into a glass and serve immediately. You may want to eat this with a spoon.

The Juiceman's Power of Juicing

271

Q: What is your overall advice for juicing success?

A: The best advice I can give you is to set a specific time to juice and be consistent. Do it first thing in the morning and then again in the afternoon. If you work away from home, have fresh juice when you come home. Drink freshly made juices before meals to help curb your appetite.

The most practical advice I can offer is to clean and dry the produce when you come home from the market. Do not wait to do this until you want to juice. If the food is washed and ready when you are ready to juice it, the odds of staying with a diet incorporating a lot of fresh juices increase dramatically. Be sure to use a biodegradable, natural cleanser available at health food stores to clean any produce that is not organically grown.

And, finally, clean your juicer well after each juicing session. The pulp can start to smell and fruit flies will appear out of nowhere. A clean juicer beckons more appealingly than a dirty one. And that, my friends, is the whole point.

Further Reading

Airola, Paavo O., N.D., Ph.D. *How to Keep Slim, Healthy and Young with Juice Fasting.* Sherwood, Oreg.: Health Plus, 1971.

Brody, Jane. *Jane Brody's Good Food Book.* New York: W. W. Norton & Company, Inc., 1985.

Carper, Jean. *The Food Pharmacy.* New York: Bantam Books, 1988.

Hendler, Sheldon Saul, M.D., Ph.D. *The Doctors' Vitamin and Mineral Encyclopedia.* New York: Simon & Schuster, 1990.

Kirschner, H. E., M.D. *Live Food Juices.* Monrovia, Calif.: H. E. Kirschner Publications, 1957.

Lee, William H., R.Ph., Ph.D. *The Book of Raw Fruit and Vegetable Juices and Drinks.* New Canaan, Conn.: Keats Publishing, Inc., 1982.

McGee, Harold. *On Food and Cooking.* New York: Charles Scribner's Sons, 1984.

Mayo Clinic. *Mayo Clinic Family Health Book: The Ultimate Illustrated Home Medical Reference.* New York: William Morrow & Co., Inc., 1990.

Murdich, Jack. *Buying Produce.* New York: Hearst Books, 1986.

Pennington, Jean A. T. *Food Values of Portions Commonly Used.* New York: Harper & Row, 1989.

Robbins, John. *Diet for a New America.* Walpole, N.H.: Stillpoint Publishing, 1987.

Schneider, Elizabeth. *Uncommon Fruits & Vegetables.* New York: Harper & Row, 1986.

Walker, Norman W., D.Sc., Ph.D. *Become Younger.* Prescott, Ariz.: Norwalk Press, 1949; rev. ed. 1978.

———. *Fresh Vegetable and Fruit Juices.* Prescott, Ariz.: Norwalk Press, 1970.

———. *The Natural Way to Vibrant Health.* Prescott Ariz.: Norwalk Press, 1972.

———. *Pure and Simple Natural Weight Control.* Prescott, Ariz.: Norwalk Press, 1981.

———. *The Vegetarian Guide to Diet & Salad.* Prescott, Ariz.: Norwalk Press, 1971.

INDEX

For ease of identification, drink ingredients and recipes in subentries appear in **bold** type.

Index

Index

Index